FROM THE
SHADOWS
TO THE
SAVIOR

CHRIST IN THE OLD TESTAMENT

Douglas Van Dorn

FROM THE
SHADOWS
TO THE
SAVIOR

CHRIST IN THE OLD TESTAMENT

Douglas Van Dorn

Waters of Creation Publishing

1614 Westin Drive, Erie, Colorado 80516

Unless otherwise noted, references are from the *English Standard Version* (ESV) of the Bible.

Cover Concept: Sarah Flashing who won the Facebook contest out of a dozen or so entries

ISBN-13:978-0-9862376-2-1 (Waters of Creation Pub.)
ISBN-10: 0986237620

Contents

Forewords

CHRIST IN THE OLD TESTAMENT? It doesn't take a seminary degree to know that Jesus wasn't born until just prior to the first century. In fact, the Bible doesn't even deal with Jesus' birth until the book of Matthew in the New Testament! Or, perhaps we've been reading it wrong this whole time…

Pastor Van Dorn has provided a marvelous introduction to a study of Christ in the Old Testament. The eternal Logos always has been and forever will be the second member of the Trinity, so shouldn't we expect to see him at work throughout all of redemptive history? Even Jesus himself made clear to some very confused disciples that he was the one they had been reading about all along (Luke 24:27, 44-47). Jesus said in John 5:39, "You [Jewish people] diligently study the Scriptures [which at that time were the 39 books of the Old Testament]…These are the Scriptures that testify about me."

Most Christians today assume the Old Testament patriarchs heard booming voices from heaven and had numerous dreams and visions directed by God for their instruction and wisdom. And while these instances surely occurred, when we look a little closer we see more to the story. Have you ever considered that just maybe God was with the people, face-to-face?

The Old Testament Scriptures are just as much about Jesus as the New. Pastor Van Dorn provides convincing, biblical evidence that unveils the identity of the Angel of the Lord, the one who the ancient Jews called the second voice in heaven, and who the Bible (more often than you might realize) refers to as the Logos of God. As you take the journey to discover Christ in the Old Testament, you will delight in the seamless continuity and progressive revelation of the entirety of Scripture. May your affections for Jesus be stirred up all the more as you discover the second person on every page of Scripture!

Pastor Nick Kennicott ~ Ephesus Church of Rincon, GA

*** *** ***

To and for a Christian, there can be nothing more important than Christ Himself. At least that's the way it *ought* to be. How many of us at some point or another have either heard the song, "You Are My All In All", or sang it ourselves? Yet, is it true? Is Jesus *really* our All in All – even in the Old Testament? One would think, that for a Christian, seeing Jesus in the book that He authored would be easy enough. Sadly, for many, not only is it difficult, but it's sometimes even sneered at. The very thought is even addressed as if it's some sort of insult to mention Jesus in the context of the Old Testament unless something very specific about Him is mentioned in the New Testament regarding it. Instead of rejoicing to find the Savior throughout all of Scripture – especially the Old Testament -, oftentimes we act like the Sheriff of Nottingham chasing Robin Hood through Sherwood Forest. We *think* the bandit might be among the trees somewhere, but at most He appears as a ghost or legend.

When did we move away from the hermeneutic that Jesus Himself used? (Himself BEING the key hermeneutic) Without Jesus, there IS no Old Testament. This is what makes the book you are about to read so important. Can you imagine seeing Hamlet, without Hamlet? Or how interesting would "The Phantom of the Opera" be without the phantom? Why then would we take the main character in God's Story, and remove Him? In God's book, we find God, and not just a general reference to some general higher power, but the Tri-une personal God – The Father, The Son, & The Holy Spirit. But what does it say when we view over half of scripture as missing the second Person of the Trinity? This is what Doug's book does so well. In all and every aspect, he shows us the Lord of the Book in all His glory.

Worship, power, The Angel of the Lord, The Right Arm of God, The Son of God, The Very Word of God, The Law of God – all of this and more is both eloquently, and concretely discussed regarding Jesus Christ. In our present time, when so many are turning the Old Testament into Aesop's Fables, or disregarding it all together, a more important volume couldn't have been written. If the point of the Old Testament was to lead to Jesus, why wouldn't we find Him IN the Old Testament? Doug answers this wholeheartedly by showing us how hard it is to NOT see Him there.

Some books aren't worth reading. Some are worth reading once. Others are worth reading time and again, and this is one of those books. Immerse yourself among the giant trees here, and see how each one shows us the Savior, making up the grand forest view of God's redemptive history. I am grateful for such a heart as Doug's in wanting to portray Jesus as all of Scripture does. Hear the Savior's voice, see the Christ's types, and read the words about Him – He who is the author of our faith. A faith that was given to us, not to conceal the Savior, but to reveal the Savior to us more and more, as we read the *entire* Bible.

Sean Kielian, ~ former elder, Reformed Baptist Church, CO

Preface

THIS SHORT BOOK ORIGINATED IN a series of blogs done for the Decablog. After reading that series, several people approached me with putting it into a single offline format that could be given or recommend to others. This is my attempt at a very basic introduction into the potentially volume filling, but certainly life-transforming subject of Christ in the Old Testament (OT).

It is divided into thirteen parts (one of which was originally a two part post). I'll refer to them as chapters in the book. After an introduction to the topic, we talk about some New Testament (NT) passages that talk explicitly about Christ or Jesus in the OT *as a person*. The next three parts focus on Christ in the OT through various concepts such as *prophecy*, *typology*, and the *law*. The next seven parts look at different words that show us the person of Christ as he is found in the OT. Christians understood many of them to talk about Christ specifically, while even early Jews understood them to be mysteriously talking about a kind of plurality within a Godhead, a fact little known to Jews or Christians in our day. The final part is a conclusion that uses Hebrews to pull these various threads together.

It is my sincere hope and prayer that this book will find a wide readership, because the contents that lay herein are of the utmost importance and value in the continuing discussion of Christ in the Old Testament, a topic so important that Jesus says through it we have life.

Doug Van Dorn ~ Reformed Baptist Church of Northern Colorado (Spring, 2015)

Dedicated to:

Uncle Norman and all my other uncles and aunts—each of whom God has graciously seen fit to savingly reveal his Son.

Part I

Introduction

Introduction

I want to look at what I believe is the key to reading the Scriptures properly. It is the key because no matter what other grid Christians may use to make the Scriptures cohere (covenant, kingdom, divine council, dispensations, etc), this one was taught explicitly by the Lord Jesus himself as the one that leads us directly to eternal life. This makes our subject very important.

That key is to see the Second Person of the Trinity throughout the Old Testament. "You search the Scriptures because you think that in them you have eternal life," Jesus told the Pharisees. But, "It is <u>they</u> that <u>bear witness</u> about <u>me</u>" (John 5:39). Yet, it is not enough to read the Scripture with him at the center. We must *come to him* because of it. He continues, "Yet you refuse to <u>come to me</u> that you may have life" (John 5:40). My hope and prayer is that as we travel down this road, you will be challenged anew to do as Jesus said. Come to him that you may have life.

The book will proceed as follows. Part I: Introduction; Part II: The NT Passages and Reflections; Part III: Christ in Prophecy; Part IV: Christ in Typology; Part V: Christ in The Law; Part VI: Christ: The Angel of the LORD; Part VII: Christ: The Word of God; Part VIII: Christ: The Name of the LORD; Part IX: Christ: The Wisdom of God; Part X: Christ: The Son of God; Part XI: Christ: The Glory of God; Part XII: Christ: The Right Arm of the God; Part XIII: Conclusions.

The Emmaus Road

After the Resurrection, two disciples of Jesus were walking from Jerusalem to a small village called Emmaus. They were talking about reports of an incredible event that they did not believe. Some were saying that Jesus had actually risen from the grave. Suddenly, the Lord Jesus himself stood behind them. Prevented from recognizing who he was, he began to scold them for being so slow to believe. The basis? "'Was it not necessary that the Christ should suffer these things and enter into his glory?' And beginning with Moses and all the Prophets, he interpreted to them in all the Scriptures the things concerning himself" (Luke 24:26-27).

The word "interpreted" here is *diermeneuo*. We derive the English word "hermeneutics" from this. Hermeneutics is the art and science of biblical interpretation.

A few years ago I was talking with a friend and I asked him, "Where do you get your hermeneutic?" He was bewildered, because his answer was not from Scripture, but from seminary. Yet, here is an explicitly taught hermeneutic from the Lord himself. This hermeneutic was to see him in and throughout the OT. This is such an important idea for Luke that he repeats it. "'These are my words that I spoke to you while I was still with you, that everything written <u>about me</u> in the <u>Law</u> of Moses and the <u>Prophets</u> and the <u>Psalms</u> must be fulfilled.' Then he opened their minds to understand the Scriptures" (Luke 24:44-45). "Moses and all the Prophets" or "the Law of Moses and the Prophets and the Psalms" are two ways of saying "the whole Old Testament." Christ is found everywhere in the Old Testament.

Now, notice the source of Jesus' consternation. They did not believe the Scriptures concerning *him*. "O foolish ones, and slow of heart to believe all that the prophets have spoken! Was it not necessary that the Christ should suffer these things and enter into his glory?" (Luke 24:25-26). To put this more bluntly, Jesus *expected* that they would read the Scriptures this way. It was not that canonically inspired Apostles were the first and only ones allowed to interpret the Old Testament with Jesus in mind, because to do so would be a dangerous speculative undertaking for anyone else to attempt. No. His expectation was that all of his disciples would have learned by now to read Scripture this way, even as Simeon and Anna had done at his birth when they alluded to Isaiah 8:14-15, 28:16, and 52:8-10 respectively in their blessings of the Christ child (see Luke 2:34, 38).[1] Next, we will look at several places where the New Testament uses just this kind of interpretation.

[1] See David W. Pao and Eckhard J. Schnabel, "Luke," in G. K. Beale and D. A. Carson, *Commentary on the New Testament Use of the Old Testament* (Grand Rapids, MI; Nottingham, UK: Baker Academic; Apollos, 2007), 273-74.

Study Questions:

1. What two chapters were cited that show Jesus teaching others how to read the Old Testament?

2. What does the word "hermeneutic" mean?

3. Does Jesus give us a hermeneutic for reading the Bible? If so, what is it?

4. Did Jesus expect that others would interpret the Scripture his way? How do you know?

PART II
NT Passages and Reflections

The NT has some pretty amazing things to say about Christ in the OT. Speaking of Israel in the wilderness, the Apostle Paul says, "All drank the same spiritual drink. For they drank from the spiritual Rock that followed them, and the <u>Rock was Christ</u>" (1Co 10:4). The Author of Hebrews says of Moses, "He considered <u>the reproach of Christ</u> greater wealth than the treasures of Egypt, for he was looking to the reward" (Heb 11:26). Jude, the half-brother of Jesus says, "I want to remind you, although you once fully knew it, that <u>Jesus, who saved a people</u> out of the land of Egypt, afterward destroyed those who did not believe" (Jude 1:5).[2]

---

[2] "Jesus" is a textual variant. "Lord" (Kurios) is the other option. Metzger says "Critical principles seem to require the adoption of 'Iesous [Jesus], which is the best attested reading among Greek and versional witnesses." Bruce Manning Metzger, United Bible Societies, *A Textual Commentary on the Greek New Testament, Second Edition a Companion Volume to the United Bible Societies' Greek New Testament (4th Rev. Ed.)* (London; New York: United Bible Societies, 1994), 657.

The Apostle John says, "Isaiah said these things because he saw [Christ's] glory and spoke of him" (John 12:41). One more will suffice to make our point. Jesus himself says, "Your father Abraham rejoiced that he would see my day. He saw it and was glad" (John 8:56).

Though the next three chapters will focus on Christ in the OT through prophecy, typology, and law, also vitally important and fundamental is the idea that Christ was himself *in* the OT as a person, not just an idea. That is what each of these five inspired men teach in one way or another. *Christ* was the Water Israel drank and the Rock that followed them. Moses did not want to disappoint *Christ*. *Jesus* saved the people out of Egypt. Isaiah saw *Christ*. Abraham saw *Jesus'* day. How could this possibly be? It is because Christianity teaches that Jesus Christ is both man and God. The human nature of Jesus Christ came into existence in Mary's womb, but the Second Person of the Trinity did not. We will look at this idea much more in later chapters in some very particular and perhaps even shocking ways.

Some Questions

For now, I want to finish with a couple of questions. Does your theology of the Second Person of the Trinity allow for him to actually *be in* the OT? If the answer is "yes," then have you been looking for him there? Many people read the OT as

---

A similar variant is found in the 1 Corinthians 10 passage (vs. 9), above. That one reads "Christ" rather than "Jesus," But "Lord" is the other option. For more, see my sermon on this passage, "I Feel Fine."

they might read Aesop's Fables to their children: great stories with a moral ending to help us be better people. Others come to the OT as if it were a divinely revealed leadership, coaching, psychology, science, and even dietary and cooking handbook. Still others have become so bored with it that they no longer read it at all. Christ in the OT is a way beyond the pure moralism, "how-to" manuals, or sheer defeatism. For when he is seen as actually being there with those people, suddenly we can say that those with faith came to him that they might have life (John 5:40). What a profoundly thrilling thought.

People were saved by Jesus in the OT.

Study Questions:

1. What five NT passages were cited as teaching that Jesus is in the OT?

2. What does 1 Corinthians 10 teach us about Christ?

3. What does Hebrews 11:26 teach us about Moses?

4. Jude 1:5 says that Jesus saved a people out of Egypt. Different copies say it was "the Lord." What is the difference in how you understand "Jesus" vs. "the Lord," and why do you suppose a copiest might be uncomfortable with the original word "Jesus?"

5. Does the idea that Jesus saved people out of Egypt make you uncomfortable? If so, why?

6. What did Isaiah see in John 12:41?

7. What was Abraham rejoicing to see in John 8:56?

PART III
Christ in Prophecy

Now we will begin to look at some specific ways that we see Christ in the OT. The first is through prophecy. Prophecy is a word from God about something that will take place in the future. This is perhaps the most well known way of seeing Christ in the OT, and it is the easiest to wrap our minds around for that reason (though the idea of prophecy itself is actually a deep mystery). That makes it a good place to start. Peter says, "God foretold by the mouth of all the prophets, that his Christ would suffer" (Acts 3:18). The word "all" (*panton*) is actually in the Greek text, and as such it makes for a stunning claim—*all the prophets* talked about Christ. This idea certainly fits with what Jesus himself taught the disciples on the road to Emmaus (see the Introduction). Let's look at a few examples.

Isaiah refers to a "suffering servant." The heart and soul of the prophecies about this Suffering One are found in Isaiah 53. "He was despised and rejected by men; a man of sorrows, and acquainted with grief ... he was despised ... he has borne our griefs and carried our sorrows ... we esteemed him stricken, smitten by God, and afflicted ... he was pierced for our transgressions; he was crushed for our iniquities" (Isa

53:3-5). While the Jews came to interpret this as referring to the nation, it is clear that the prophet has an individual in mind, and the NT cites verses from this chapter in all four Gospels, Acts, Romans, 1 Peter, 1 John and other books. Each time, they say it is fulfilled in the person of Jesus Christ. Other prophets talk about Christ's suffering too. In a passage badly misinterpreted by some, *Daniel* says that Messiah is "cut off" (Dan 9:26), referring to the crucifixion. *Zechariah* talks about Christ's being pierced on the cross (Zech 12:10). *David* goes into great detail about the sufferings of Christ (Ps 22).

But there are other prophecies as well. *Micah* says he would be born in Bethlehem (Mic 5:2). Isaiah says he would be born of a virgin (Isa 7:14). *Hosea* says he would be called out of Egypt (Hos 11:1). *Jeremiah* talks about the weeping concerning the death of the babies when Herod tried to kill the Christ (Jer 31:15). *Malachi* predicted the messenger John who came to announce the Messiah (Mal 3:1). *Joel* predicted Christ sending the Holy Spirit (Joel 2:28-32). *Moses* foresaw Christ being the greatest prophet (Deut 18:15-19). The Apostle Paul uses *Habakkuk* as a summary of the whole work of Christ saying, "I am doing a work in your days that you would not believe if told" (Hab 1:5; cf. Acts 13:41).

These are not the generic, statistically possible predictions of a horoscope, or the mumbling riddles of a Nostradamus that could mean just about anything. They are specific, clear, intelligible, and statistically impossible to occur by chance in the life of a single individual. All of these things were predicted centuries prior to their taking place in history, and the

NT teaches us to be looking for Christ through prophecy wherever prophecy is to be found.

Prophecies do at least a couple of things. First, they prove that what took place in the days of Jesus was really and truly from God. "Who is like me," asks the LORD. "Let him proclaim it. Let him declare and set it before me, since I appointed an ancient people. Let them declare what is to come, and what will happen" (Isa 44:7). The point is, only God knows the future.

Second, prophecy is relevant to faith. Now, prophecy does not *creature* faith. Jesus records that Abraham said, "They have Moses and the Prophets; let them hear them ... If they do not hear Moses and the Prophets, neither will they be convinced if someone should rise from the dead" (Luke 16:29, 31). Jesus himself said, "If you believed Moses, you would believe me; for he wrote of me" (John 5:46). But prophecies do *strengthen* our faith. "Concerning this salvation, the prophets who prophesied about the grace that was to be yours searched and inquired carefully, inquiring what person or time the Spirit of Christ in them was indicating when he predicted the sufferings of Christ and the subsequent glories" (1 Pet 1:10-11).

Perhaps the first and greatest of all these prophecies comes in the Garden of Eden. "I will put enmity between you [Satan] and the woman, and between your offspring and her offspring; he [Christ] shall bruise your head, and you shall bruise his heel" (Gen 3:15). This prophecy has a multilevel fulfillment. At the cross, Satan bruised Christ's heel. At the same time, and through the resurrection and ascension, Christ crushed Satan's head. And very soon, "The God of peace will … crush Satan under your feet. The grace of our Lord Jesus Christ be with you" (Rom 16:20).

Study Questions:

1. What is Prophecy?

2. What does Acts 3:18 teach us about prophecy?

3. What Prophecies about Christ come to your mind when thinking about the question of prophecy in the OT?

4. What is the content of the first prophecy in the Bible (Gen 3:15)?

PART IV
Christ in Typology

We have observed how Christ is seen in the OT through prophecy. Now, we want to look at how he is seen through something called typology. Typology is basically a heavenly, eternal archetype (an original that is copied for some purpose) built into redemptive-historical persons, places, or things by God. As an analogy, think of a copper planchet used at a

mint. The planchet is literally struck or smashed with the imprint of Abraham Lincoln to become a penny. Or think of an old typewriter, where the image of a letter is struck onto a piece of paper. These

are "types." Obviously, you can only have a type if the archetype already exists. Christ is the archetype who is "struck" into OT persons, places, and things. This idea is a bit less understood than prophecy, but it just as important.

The Greek word is *tupos*. It is a rather rare word, but when it is used, it is powerful in meaning. The OT LXX (Septuagint, that is the Greek translation of the Hebrew) has Moses telling the workers of the tabernacle, "See, you shall make them according to the <u>pattern</u> (*tupos*) showed you in the mount" (Ex

25:40). Hebrews comments on this verse saying, "They serve a <u>copy</u> and shadow of heavenly things" (Heb 8:5). The tabernacle had to be replicated exactly as commanded, because it was a visible, created copy of the heavenly invisible temple. The tabernacle was a type (model, copy, and shadow) of the heavenly temple. It was not the heavenly temple itself, but a replica that mysteriously brought the people to the heavenly counterpart.

The accompanying drawing (see below) is my own modification of one developed (as far as I can tell) by Geerhardus Vos.

All of the things in and about the tabernacle were types of the heavenly reality. This included things like the sacrificial animals and the priests who offered them. These animals were types of Christ, for he is the "<u>Lamb</u> of God who takes away the sin of the world" (John 1:29). His was a "better sacrifice" (Heb 9:23). His was a better priesthood (Heb 5:10). He was a better priest, because he was without sin (Heb 4:15). His offering was in a better temple (Matt 12:6), in heaven itself (Heb 9:24), as he is the temple of heaven (John 2:21). Therefore, his was a "better ministry" (Heb 8:6) and a better covenant (Heb 7:22), for the old covenant was a type of the new covenant. In these ways and more, the OT shadows and types were given to people to

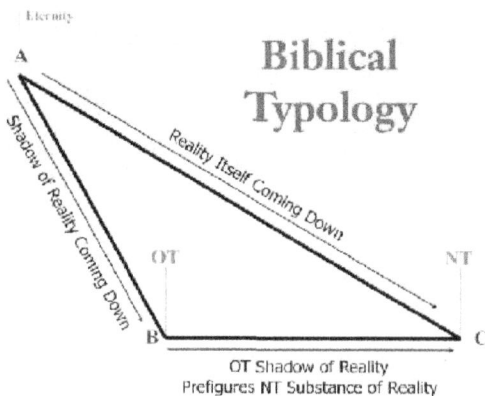

Biblical Typology

Eternity

A

Shadow of Reality Coming Down

Reality Itself Coming Down

OT

NT

B

C

OT Shadow of Reality
Prefigures NT Substance of Reality

point forward (and backward) to a heavenly origin and a future fulfillment in someone who would fulfill their purposes.

Sometimes, people in the OT can be viewed the same way. The Apostle says that Adam "was a type (*tupos*) of the one who was to come" (Rom 5:14). So, Jesus is called the "second man" (1 Cor 15:47) and "last Adam" (1 Cor 15:45). What is that type? "For as in Adam all die, so also in Christ shall all be made alive" (1 Cor 15:22). Adam's son Abel was also a type. Abel's death was a sacrifice likened to Jesus' own sacrifice which is "better" (Heb 12:24). So Jesus is a greater Abel, as both were put to death for their righteousness. Jesus says, "They repented at the preaching of Jonah, and behold, something greater than Jonah is here" (Matt 12:41) and the Queen of Sheba "came from the ends of the earth to hear the wisdom of Solomon, and behold, something greater than Solomon is here" (Matt 12:42). Jesus is here a greater preacher who has a greater sign (three days in the earth) than Jonah, and who is full of greater wisdom than Solomon. Both men are viewed as types of Christ in these ways.

Things and events can also be viewed typologically. Christ says he is the manna that comes down from heaven (John 6:51). Peter tells us, Christian baptism is said to correspond (*antitupos*) to the Flood-baptism (1 Pet 3:20-21). Paul says, "I do not want you to be unaware, brothers, that our fathers were all under the cloud, and all passed through the sea, and all were baptized into Moses in the cloud and in the sea, and all ate the same spiritual food, and all drank the same spiritual drink. For they drank from the spiritual Rock that followed them, and the Rock was Christ" (1 Cor 10:1-4). A couple of verses later he adds that the many events of the exodus "took place as examples (*tupos*) for us, that we might not desire evil as they did" (1 Cor 10:6). This last type is ethical in nature, yet it is still rooted in Christ: "We must not put Christ to the test, as some of them did" (1 Cor 10:9 ESV).

We should understand from these many examples that seeing Christ in typology is more complicated than making some arbitrary and forced connections as some have done. A good example of finding a wrong type can be found in the early church where it was common to see the scarlet thread of Rahab as a type of Christ's blood—because it was red. This is wrong because there is no immediately recognizable correspondence between Rahab's thread and Christ's blood.

Rather, biblical types are related to one another organically and substantially (to the substance) rather than accidentally (an attribute that does not affect the substance like "redness"): temple to Heavenly Temple, wisdom to Wisdom, three days to three days, man to Man, Israel's grumbling to our own grumbling, and so on. While not always easy to identify proper types or to apply them correctly, nevertheless, we need to be reading the OT as the shadowy pattern of things to come that it is, for all of the OT, in one way or another, finds its fulfillment in Him.

Study Questions:

1. Define "typology."

2. What kinds of things can be "types" in Scripture?

3. List at least three passages in the NT that cite an OT type.

4. How might typology be similar to prophecy?

5. Why is typology important to a study of Christ in the OT?

6. List some specific OT types that Jesus fulfills.

PART V
Christ and the Law

One of the chief concerns of the OT is to make sure that God's people know about righteousness and morality. Righteousness and morality come to us through "law." I am a Reformed Christian. Many Reformed people hold to things called confessions of faith. These were how the Protestants formally differentiated themselves from Roman Catholics at the beginning of the Reformation. They set up positive, robust statements of what they believed about the Bible.

My own confession teaches that the law of God can be divided into three parts: moral, civil, and ceremonial (*London Baptist Confession* 19.3-4). The moral law is summarized in the Ten Commandments, and the other two kinds of law take up much of Exodus, Leviticus, and Deuteronomy. Now is not the time to get into how these distinctions work, other than to say that in the last chapter we saw some examples of how ceremonial law (i.e. sacrifices, temples, etc.) are fulfilled in Christ via typology. In this chapter, we want to focus on how Christ is seen in, especially, the moral law.

The first thing I want to take notice of is that Christ himself was the Giver of the Commandments to Moses. Both Stephen and Paul say that the Law was put into effect through angels (Acts 7:53; Gal 3:19; cf. Deut 33:2 LXX[3]). But Paul adds something interesting. He says that there was an intermediary here. "An intermediary implies more than one, but God is one" (Gal 3:20). Since angels and God are the only two beings mentioned, it would seem that the intermediary is between them. If so, this would mean that Moses can't be in mind, because as a man, he is below angels (for now; cf. Ps 8:5).[4] That is, he would mediate between humans and God, not angels and God. This otherwise inexplicable verse is cleared up when we understand that it is possible for such an intermediary to exist, since there is both unity and *plurality* in the Godhead. I believe the intermediary he is talking about is Christ himself, as he is found in the figure of the Angel of the LORD.[5] We will look at this angel in a couple of chapters. For now, it is enough to say that as the Giver of the law, Christ would thus

---

[3] Michael Heiser has a short summary of the differences between the LXX and the Hebrew text. See Michael Heiser, "Why Use the Septuagint," *Logos Talk* (Dec 2007), https://blog.logos.com/2007/12/why_use_the_septuagint/, last accessed 5-4-2015.

[4] For the difficulties on this mediator being Moses see F. F. Bruce, *The Epistle to the Galatians: a Commentary on the Greek Text*, New International Greek Testament Commentary (Grand Rapids, MI: W.B. Eerdmans Pub. Co., 1982), 175-80.

[5] See Michael Heiser, *The Myth That is True*, unpublished. (This book is soon to be published under two different names, one as an academic book called *The Unseen Realm*, the other for lay people called *Supernatural*).

be in the OT in a profound way. It is why, if I were able to create my own red-letter edition of the Bible, that the entire Bible would be in red-letters, especially the OT law.

This becomes important when considering Christ and the Law from another viewpoint. It is the vista that he himself shows us in his Sermon on the Mount. Before preaching the greatest sermon ever on the moral law, Jesus begins by saying, "Do not think that I have come to abolish the Law or the Prophets; I have not come to abolish them but to fulfill them" (Matt 5:17). Up to this point in Matthew's book, every time the word "fulfill" has been used, it has meant that Jesus fulfills something from the OT (Matt 1:22; 2:5; 15, 17, 23 etc.), especially a prophecy or a type. In one of these instances, he is baptized in order to "fulfill all righteousness" (Matt 3:15). There is a typological aspect to this fulfillment, but it is more even than that.[6] According to Deuteronomy 6:25, "righteousness" is directly linked to obeying the Law. "And it will be righteousness for us, if we are careful to do all this commandment before the LORD our God, as he has commanded us." In Matthew's Gospel, it refers to good works or obedience (3:15; 5:10, 20; 6:1; 21:32).[7]

Many people have been deeply confused about what Jesus is doing in the Sermon on the Mount. Many think he is abol-

---

[6] See my book *Waters of Creation: A Biblical-Theological Study of Baptism* (Erie, Co: Waters of Creation Pub., 2009), 13-23.

[7] See Michael Goulder, *Midrash and Lection in Matthew: The Speaker's Lectures in Biblical Studies, 1969-71* (London: SPCK, 1974), 262 and also my Waters of Creation, 11-12.

ishing the law, overthrowing the OT law, intensifying old law, or putting "love" in as the great new law. Some even think he is a different god than the God of the OT, which is why understanding that he was the original giver of the law is so important. None of these things are true.[8] What Jesus is doing is teaching people:

1. What the law has always said,
2. Contrasted with what the Pharisees were teaching that it said,
3. In order to show that no man can keep the law perfectly (which the Pharisees were basically saying that they were doing),
4. Except for the One who "fulfills the law," who is Christ himself.

In other words, the way we find Jesus in the moral law is to see that:

1. He is the original Law-Giver.
2. This law reflects God's (and therefore Christ's) holy perfect state of being.
3. Therefore, the law needs to be kept perfectly in order to inherit eternal life (this is the idea of the Covenant of Works).
4. Christ obeyed the law perfectly as a man, so that he might become a greater mediator than the OT prophets and priests (this is the idea of the Covenant of Grace).

---

[8] See especially Greg Welty, "Eschatological Fulfillment and the Confirmation of Mosaic Law," last accessed 8-14-2014; William Hendriksen and Simon J. Kistemaker, *Exposition of the Gospel According to Matthew*, vol. 9, New Testament Commentary (Grand Rapids: Baker Book House, 1953–2001), 288-383, and my sermon series on the Sermon on the Mount.

His sinlessness (Heb 4:15) is the fulfillment of the law of God. The law was a tutor to lead us to Christ (Gal 3:24).

With these lenses, suddenly we can find that reading those most tedious and (some think) boring parts of the OT—the Law of God—can be done in a way that points us beyond those laws to the one who gives us life through faith in his law-keeping done on our behalf. And this ought to make us profoundly grateful people that God does not require our own perfect obedience in order to have eternal life, while ironically, through this new life and the Holy Spirit, creating in us new desires to keep and obey the very law–the law that was not abolished or passed away–that once held us captive to Satan through sin.

Study Questions:

1. What are the three divisions of "law?"

2. What was said about the mediary between God and angels (Gal 3:20)?

3. Jesus said he came to "fulfill" the law (Matt 5:17). What does "fulfill" mean?

4. The chapter listed four things that show us "the way we find Jesus in the moral law." What are they?

PART VI

Christ: The Angel of the LORD

In the next several chapters we will turn our attention away from Christ in the OT as he is found in more general ways like prophecy, types, and law, towards Christ as he is literally in the OT as a person or figure in Israel. We will do this first, by looking at a particular individual that Geerhardus Vos calls, "The most important and characteristic form of revelation in the patriarchal period."[9] Then we will turn our attention to various words that came to be understood by Jews (at least for a time) and early Christians that were, for lack of a better term, hypostatically linked to this individual in the Old Testament.

The individual in mind here is the Angel of the LORD. Let's return to this idea of Jude that "Jesus saved a people out of Egypt." Where does he get this from? Well, he isn't just making it up. Rather, it comes from places like Exodus 23:20-21. "Behold, I send an angel before you to guard you on the way and to bring you to the place that I have prepared. Pay careful attention to him and obey his voice; do not rebel against him, for he will not pardon your transgression, for my name is in him." Let's begin to unpack this a bit.

---

[9] Geerhardus Vos, *Biblical Theology* (Grand Rapids, MI: Eerdmans, 1977), 72.

"The Angel of the LORD" appears with this exact title many times in the OT. He comes explicitly to Hagar (Gen 16:7ff), Abraham (Gen 22:11ff), Moses (Ex 3:2ff), Balaam (Num 22:22ff), Israel (Jdg 2:1ff), Gideon (Jdg 6:21ff), Manoah (Jdg 13:3ff), Elijah (1 Kgs 19:7ff), Zechariah (Zech 1:11ff), and others. Perhaps the most important (and least remembered) is his first appearance to Moses.

The Burning Bush

The Angel appears to Moses in the Burning Bush. We need to look carefully at the language. "And the angel of the LORD appeared to him in a flame of fire out of the midst of a bush" (Ex 3:2). There is an angel in the fire (the fire likely being an image of the Holy Spirit).[10] After Moses turns aside to look at this amazing sight (vs. 3) it says, "When the LORD saw that he turned aside to see, God called to him out of the bush" (vs. 4). Here then, the Angel of the LORD is called both LORD (Yahweh) and God (Elohim). This is very similar to what After telling him to take his sandals off

---

[10] See Meredith Kline, *Images of the Spirit* (Eugene, OR: Wipf & Stock, 1999), 17-20, 72-73.

because the ground is holy (vs. 5), the angel of the LORD, still speaking, says, "I am the God of your father, the God of Abraham, the God of Isaac, and the God of Jacob." And Moses hid his face for he "was afraid to look at God" (vs. 6). He was afraid to look at God because he could see God in some sense, that is the Angel of God. After a short conversation, Moses asks the Angel of the LORD his name. The Angel says to call him "I AM WHO I AM" (vs. 14) and "Yahweh, the God of your fathers" (vs. 15). Many people have not recognized that all of this is the angel speaking from the bush, and thus they default to the abstract word "theophany" when trying to explain it. In reality this is the same person who called himself "I AM" throughout the Gospel of John. In taking this title upon himself, Jesus is claiming to be the Angel in the bush.

Gideon

A second story that shows us this interaction between the Angel and the name of God takes place with Gideon. It begins, "Now the angel of the LORD came and sat under the terebinth at Ophrah ... while ... Gideon was beating out wheat in the winepress" (Jdg 6:11). Notice the very physical language here, exactly what we would expect if it were an angel coming to talk to someone.

"And the angel of the LORD appeared to him and said to him, 'The LORD [Yahweh] is with you, O mighty man of valor.' And Gideon said to him, 'Please, sir, if the LORD is with us, why then has all this happened to us? And where are all his wonderful deeds that our fathers recounted to us, saying, 'Did not <u>the LORD bring us up from Egypt</u>?' But now the LORD has forsaken us and given us into the hand of Midian'" (12-13). Remember when we talked a moment ago about the Angel bringing the people out of Egypt? The same idea is being presented again here.

The next verse is critical. Do not miss it. "And <u>the LORD turned</u> to him <u>and said</u>, 'Go in this might of yours and save Israel from the hand of Midian; do not I send you?'" (14). Here, it explicitly calls the Angel of the LORD, Yahweh, for there is no one else here but these two people. But Gideon did not know it yet. "He said to him, 'Please, Lord [Adonai], how can I save Israel? Behold, my clan is the weakest in Manasseh, and I am the least in my father's house.' And <u>the LORD</u> said to him, 'But <u>I</u> will be with you, and you shall strike the Midianites as one man'" (15-16).

Gideon now seems to understand that someone important is talking to him. But who? "And he said to him, 'If now I have found favor in your eyes, then show me a sign that it is you who speak with me. Please do not depart from here until I come to you and bring out my present and set it before you.' And he said, 'I will stay till you return.' So Gideon went into his house and prepared a young goat and unleavened cakes from an ephah of flour. The meat he put in a basket, and the broth he put in a pot, and <u>brought them to him under the terebinth</u> and presented them. And <u>the angel of God</u> said to him, 'Take the meat and the unleavened cakes, and put them on this rock, and pour the broth over them.' And he did so.

Then the angel of the LORD reached out the tip of the staff that was in his hand and touched the meat and the unleavened cakes. And <u>fire</u> sprang up from the rock and consumed the meat and the unleavened cakes. And the angel of the LORD vanished from his sight" (17-21).

Now Gideon understands: "Then Gideon perceived that he was <u>the angel of the LORD</u>. And Gideon said, 'Alas, <u>O Lord GOD</u> [Adonai Yahweh]! For now I have seen <u>the angel of the LORD face to face</u>'" (22). This story does something that, if you begin looking, you will see happening all over the early books of the Bible. Yahweh and the Angel of Yahweh are interchangeable terms.

Someone might ask, how could the Angel *be* Yahweh? The Angel of the LORD is Yahweh's messenger, for angels are messengers. In this way, he is distinct from Yahweh (the Father). Delivering messages is the function of an angel. But the term "angel" only speaks to a function. It does not necessarily describe a being's ontology (his DNA, so to speak). Christians understand that God is both One and Three. The idea comes from the Old Testament. This is made clearer by a couple of other passages.

The Angel of the Name

The first returns us to Exodus 23:20-21. "Behold, I send an <u>angel</u> before you to guard you on the way and to bring you to the place that I have prepared. <u>Pay careful attention</u> to him and <u>obey</u> his voice; do not rebel against him, for he will not <u>pardon your transgression</u>, for my <u>name</u> is in him." Who is speaking here? My opinion is that the Angel of the LORD is speaking on behalf of Yahweh in heaven about the Angel of the LORD; or to put it into NT parlance, the Son is speaking on behalf of the Father about the Son. This is exactly what we see Jesus doing in the NT as well (cf. John 5:20-23; 10:34-38; etc), as he again identifies himself with this OT Person.

Another important passage to look at is Judges 2:1-5. It helps inform the previous text. "Now the Angel of the LORD went up from Gilgal to Bochim. And he said, 'I brought you up from Egypt and brought you into the land that I swore to give to your fathers. I said, 'I will never break my covenant with you, and you shall make no covenant with the inhabitants of this land; you shall break down their altars.' But you have not obeyed my voice. What is this you have done? So now I say, I will not drive them out before you, but they shall become thorns in your sides, and their gods shall be a snare to you.' As soon as the angel of the LORD spoke these words to all the people of Israel, the people lifted up their voices and wept. And they called the name of that place Bochim. And they sacrificed there to the LORD."

Notice two things. First, they did not obey his voice, though as we saw in Exodus 22:21, this is what they were commanded to do. Second, the Angel of the LORD is the one who covenanted with Israel. This is because the Angel is the covenant God of Israel. I think most people think much too generically about the covenant making "God," rather than the

Second Person of the Trinity who is the mediatory. Yet here it is, right in the Bible.

Jacob

Next, we see the Angel of the LORD being called "God" (*elohim*) other times besides the burning bush. For example, at Bethel it says, "The <u>angel of God</u> said to me [Jacob] in the dream … 'I am <u>the God</u> of Bethel" (Gen 31:11-12). Later, Jacob blesses Joseph and says, "<u>The God</u> before whom my fathers Abraham and Isaac walked, <u>the God</u> who has been my shepherd all my life long to this day, <u>the angel</u> who has redeemed me from all evil, bless the boys" (Gen 48:15-16).

Of this passage Calvin says, "It is necessary that Christ should be here meant, who does not bear in vain the title of Angel … he was always the bond of connection between God and man, and … For there was always so wide a distance between God and men, that, without a mediator, there could be no communication."[11]

In light of the "saving of people out of Egypt" (Jude 5), the "bringing you to the place" (Ex 23:20), and the "bringing us up from Egypt" (Jdg 6:15) that are all said of either Jesus or the Angel of the LORD, it is curious to note that Jacob says, "The angel … has redeemed me from all evil" (Gen 48:16). Though prior to the exodus, the idea of deliverance or rescu-

---

[11] Genesis 48:16. See John Calvin and John King, *Commentary on the First Book of Moses Called Genesis*, vol. 2 (Bellingham, WA: Logos Bible Software, 2010), 429.

ing or saving is the same. In fact, the word used (*go'el*) means a kinsman redeemer.

Joshua

The point is, the Angel of the LORD is called Yahweh, God, and I AM among other names that we normally associated in our minds only with "God" (the one being) or perhaps with the Father. He also covenants with Israel, fights for his people, redeems them from slavery, forgives sin, and must be obeyed. Perhaps one final thing should be mentioned here.

When he shows himself to Joshua as the commander of the army of the LORD, he tells Joshua the very same thing he told Moses, "Take off your sandals from your feet, for the place where you are standing is holy" (Josh 5:15; cf. Ex 3:5). This was in response to Joshua's "worship" (vs. 14), which the Angel accepted. Now, unless this was actually an evil fallen heavenly being, he would not have accepted worship (cf. Rev 22:9) unless he was God.

Study Questions:

1. What key OT passage was said helps us interpret Jude 5?

2. Who spoke to Moses in the burning bush? What name did he give himself?

3. What common word for God is used to help identify the Angel of the LORD in the Gideon story?

4. Who covenanted with the people at Bochim (Judges 2:1-5)?

5. What common term is used synonymously with "angel" by Jacob?

6. What figure identifies himself as the person in the Burning Bush to Joshua (Josh 5:15)?

PART VII

Christ: The Word of God

(Part I)

Now we will turn our attention to various words that are identified with the Angel in such a way that they become synonymous with Him. We begin with "the Word." The word of God can be understood in two mysteriously united senses. The first is that of God's *speech*. "Long ago, at many times and in many ways, God <u>spoke</u> to our fathers by the prophets" (Heb 1:1). These prophets put their words, their speech, down on paper which became Holy Scripture: God's word. "They received <u>the word</u> with all eagerness, examining <u>the Scriptures</u> daily to see if these things were so" (Acts 17:11).

The second way the Word of God can be understood is through God's *Son*. "In these last days he has <u>spoken</u> to us by <u>his Son</u>" (Heb 1:2). He is the Word of God. "In the beginning was the Word, and the Word was with God, and <u>the Word was God</u> … And <u>the word became flesh</u> and dwelt among us" (John 1:1, 14). Many are familiar with the Greek word for "word" here. It is *logos*. But where does John get this idea? Is he just making it up?

Before the Gospel of John was written, Philo the Jewish philosopher and historian wrote, "And even if there be not as yet anyone who is worthy to be called a <u>son of God</u>, nevertheless let him labour earnestly to be adorned according to his <u>first-born</u> *logos*, the <u>eldest of his angels</u>, as the great archangel of many names; for he is called, the authority, and <u>the name of God</u>, and <u>the Word</u> [*logos*], and <u>man</u> according to God's <u>image,</u> and he who sees Israel … Even if we are not yet suitable to be called the sons of God, still we may deserve to be called the children of his eternal image, of his most sacred logos; for the image of God is his most ancient word [logos]" (*Confusion of Tongues* 146).

Many read John against the backdrop of later Greek Gnosticism. Yet, it is clear that John 1:1ff is a reflection on the OT (Genesis 1:1ff). Also, John is a Jew, and as Philo demonstrates, there are Jewish roots for seeing a figure in the OT who is called both the Angel and the Word, and who seems to be both God and yet not God. This fact may be surprising to many readers for the simple reason that modern Judaism is utterly Unitarian. To see plurality in a "Godhead" is, for today's Jew, the ultimately blasphemy. "The LORD our, the LORD is one" (Deut 6:4). Period.

Many Christians have uncritically accepted this Unitarian view of God in the OT thinking, "No one could possibly know about a Second Person in a Godhead from the OT. Only in the NT do we see this." Never mind the Angel, or the implications of a theology that comes out of thin air like a magicians rabbit out of a hat, or that the NT was using the OT to prove this theology, which would have been utterly unconvincing if they were just making it up. In fact, scholars are starting to uncover how in Second Temple Judaism (the Judaism of Jesus' day), there were many Jews who had theological room for a Godhead. They are arguing, persuasively in my opinion, that John's *logos* should not be read exclusively or even primarily through Greek philosophy, but rather Jewish OT lenses.[12] As a result, we can start to make sense of why so many Jews were actually being convinced by the arguments of the NT and early church of a Second God-Person being right there in the history of OT peoples.

To see this, let's return to the monotheist Hellenistic Jew Philo (20 BC – c. 50 AD). Though he does not seem to have ever come into contact with Christians, and therefore never

---

[12] Cf. Alan F. Segal, *Two Powers in Heaven: Early Rabbinic Reports about Christianity and Gnosticism* (SJLA 25; Leiden: E. J. Brill, 1977); also Richard Bauckham, "The Throne of God and the Worship of Jesus," in *The Jewish Roots of Christological Monotheism: Papers from the St. Andrews Conference on the Historical Origins of the Worship of Jesus*, ed. C. Newman, J. Davila, and G. Lewis (Leiden: E. J. Brill, 1999), 43-69; Daniel Boyarin, "The Gospel of the Memra: Jewish Binitarianism and the Prologue to John," *Harvard Theological Review* 94:3 (2001): 243-84; M. J. Edwards, "Justin's Logos and the Word of God," *JECS* 3 (1995): 261-80; Larry Hurtado, "The Binitarian Shape of Early Christian Worship," in *The Jewish Roots of Christological Monotheism: Papers from the St. Andrews Conference on the Historical Origins of the Worship of Jesus* (ed. Carey C. Newman, James R. Davila, and Gladys S. Lewis; Leiden: E. J. Brill, 1999), 187-213.

became one, he nevertheless writes, "Examine it accurately, and see whether there are really two Gods ... There is one true God only ... and what he here calls God (not 'the God' but 'of God') is his most ancient *logos*" (*Dreams* 1.228-230). Yet he also says, "No mortal thing could have been formed on the similitude of the supreme Father of the universe, but only after the pattern of the second deity, who is the *logos* of the supreme Being" (*Questions on Genesis* 2.62). As we will see in Part VII, Philo was not thinking of the *logos* in terms of "logic" or "reason," or even Torah (law), but in terms of a person. So how could Philo hold that there is both one God and yet a second God [his words]?

Just here, we should point out something that his contemporary Aramaic speaking Jews were doing. As they transmitted the Holy Scripture into their own common tongue, the Jews would create "Targums." I like to think of Targums as paraphrases of the Scripture (like The Living Bible or The Message) that sometimes added Jewish tradition. Now, "*memra*" is the Aramaic equivalent of the Greek *logos*. It occurs regularly in the Torah Targums. According to one scholar, "'Memra' is used as a buffer word, introduced apparently for some theological purpose, such as to avoid anthropomorphisms, to

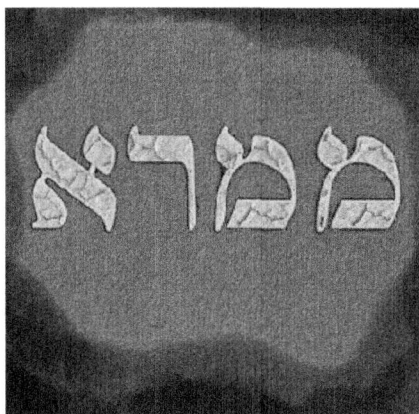

avoid making God the direct object or subject of actions connected with creation"[13]

In the Targums, "I have established my covenant between me and you" (Gen 17:7) becomes "I have established My covenant between <u>my Memra</u> and you." "They heard the sound/voice of the LORD God" (Gen 3:8) becomes, "They heard the voice <u>of the Memra</u> of the Lord God." They heard the voice of the word? Basically, Memra ends up becoming more than a personification of God. It becomes a kind of second God in the Targums, and this by monotheistic Jews. This was not Zoroastrian dualism with two equal but opposite gods (one good, one evil), but two good equal yet distinct persons of a Godhead. This seems to be a main source from which John is drawing upon his *logos* theology.

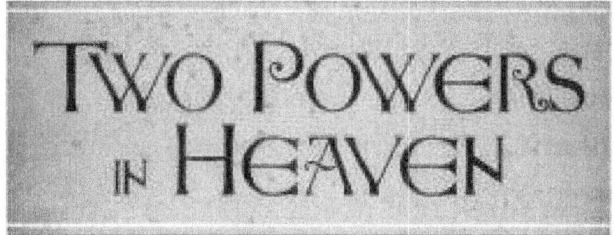

★★★

Let's now turn our attention to three fascinating passages where the Word of God becomes embodied in the OT. The Targum on Genesis 15:1 reads, "The word (*pithgama*) of the

[13] Kevin Cathcart, Michael Maher, and Martin McNamara, eds., *The Aramaic BibleA: Targum Neofiti 1: Genesis*, trans. Martin McNamara, vol. 1 (Collegeville, MN: The Liturgical Press, 1992), 38.

LORD was with Abram in a prophecy, as follows: 'Do not fear, Abram, my Memra (*memra*) shall be your strength" (Onkelos Targum Gen 15:1). Notice that there are two Aramaic words used for "word" here. The Targum is essentially separating "words" from a person, deifying the Memra as a kind of Second (good) Power in heaven. In fact, the Rabbis were using the phrase "Two Powers in Heaven."[14] This became such a problem for them because so many Jews were converting to Christianity, that the Rabbis made it a heresy sometime after the destruction of their temple in 70 AD. Judaism has been Unitarian in outlook ever since.

Abraham

The Targum seems concerned here about what may be something ever stranger in the Hebrew. A literal reading in English is, "After these things the <u>word</u> of the LORD came to Abram in a <u>vision</u>" (Gen 15:1). Pause a second to think about this. Words do not ordinarily come to eyes, but to ears. There are some curious things that happen after this. First, Abram responds to the word of the LORD with "Adonai-Yahweh" ("Lord GOD"; 15:2, 8). It is interesting to note that Adonai is the same term David uses to speak of his "Lord," a Lord who is distinct from his LORD (Yahweh) in Psalm 110:1. To put that more simply, there are three persons in the Psalm verse: Yahweh, Adonai, and David. The NT quotes or alludes to this verse in the Psalm perhaps more

---

[14] Alan F. Segal, *Two Powers in Heaven: Early Rabbinic Reports about Christianity and Gnosticism* (SJLA 25; Leiden: E. J. Brill, 1977), Introduction and pp. 33-34.

than any verse in the OT, and each time it calls this Adonai Jesus, and makes him separate from the Father.[15] So Jesus is Adonai, at least in the Psalm. Going back to Genesis, second, the word of the LORD, "brought him [Abram] outside" (vs. 5).

Is this purely figurative speech? One thing that is probably true at this point is relevant here. Abram is not yet asleep, for the text makes a point to tell us that he falls into a sleep only later on in the story (Gen 15:12). Third, the word of the LORD is simply called "Yahweh" (Jehovah, LORD; vs. 13). We actually see two Yahweh's later on in the same story (one in heaven, one on earth), in Genesis 19:24, a text that nearly every Church Father said refers to the Father and the Son.[16] Fourth, the LORD walks through pieces of dead animals. Some might suggest that it was just a smoking pot and a flaming torch that were sort of dancing through the pieces of

---

[15] Matt 22:44; 26:64; Mark 12:36; 14:62; 16:19; Luke 20:42-43; 22:69; Acts 2:34-35; Rom 8:34; 1 Cor 15:25; Eph 1:20; Col 3:1; Heb 1:3, 13; 8:1; 10:12-13; 12:2.

[16] JUSTIN MARTYR, *Dialogue* 127; PSEUDO-IGNATIUS, *Antiochians* 2; IRENAEUS, *Against Heresies* 3.6.1; TERTULLIAN, *Against Praxeas* 13; CYPRIAN, *Against the Jews* 3.33; NOVATIAN, *On the Trinity* 18.15–17; EUSEBIUS, *Ecclesiastical History* 1.2.9; ATHANASIUS, *Discourses Against the Arians* 2.15.13; HILARY OF POITIERS, *On the Trinity* 5.16; GREGORY NAZIANZEN, *Oration* 29:17; BASIL, *On Prov. 7:22*; AMBROSE, *Exposition of the Christian Faith* 1.3.22-23; CHRYSOSTOM, *Homily 3:* 2 Tim 1:13-18; AUGUSTINE, *Tractates on John* 51.3; CYRIL, *Comments on 1 John 1:2*; SOCRATES SCHOLASTICUS, *Ecclesiastical History* 2.30; *CONSTITUTIONS OF THE HOLY APOSTLES* 5.20. There were even Jews who were saying this referred to two Yahwehs. See R. Ishmael b. Yosi (170-200 C.E.), Gen 19:24 (*b. Sanh.* 38b or 4:5, V.11 A-C); *Genesis Rabbah* 51.2.

the animals like some kind of cartoonish personification. But it seems pretty clear that "The LORD" (vs. 13) is the person holding these two objects as he walks through with them.

Jeremiah

A second story is the calling of Jeremiah. It begins by saying, "Now the <u>word</u> of the LORD came to me" (Jer 1:4). The LXX has *logos*, as it does for most of prophets who have the "word of the LORD" come to them. Let's notice three things about the rest of Jeremiah's call. First, Jeremiah responds to the word by saying, "Lord GOD" (Adonai-Yahweh; vs. 6). This is identical to Abraham, except that this time the association with the "word" or *logos* is as "Lord GOD" seems explicit. Second, the text next calls "the word of the LORD," simply "the LORD" (Yahweh; Jer 1:7, 9). "The word of the LORD came to me" (vs. 4) becomes "the LORD said" (vs. 7). Many people miss these subtleties of the text, but the NT authors sure didn't. Putting that another way, it is very possible to take this as saying that the word of the LORD is the LORD. Third, it says the LORD "put out <u>his hand</u> and <u>touched my mouth</u>" (1:9).

Samuel

The third story is the call of Samuel. It begins, "The <u>word</u> of the LORD was rare in those days; there was no frequent <u>vision</u>" (1 Sam 3:1). Here we have the word associated with a vision again, and this is common among all the prophets. Then it gives us the strange detail that Eli's eyes had begun to grow dim (vs. 2). This is not referring to his "spiritual" sight.

The man was literally going blind. This little detail about Eli seems clearly related to the word coming to the eyes in visions. But first, the word of the LORD is called Yahweh again (4). As one would expect, he speaks to Samuel (three times). But it tells us that Samuel did not recognize the LORD because "he did not yet know the LORD, and the word of the LORD had not yet been revealed to him" (vs. 7). Finally, to get his attention, "The LORD came and stood, calling as at other times" (vs. 10). Apparently, Eli could not help Samuel figure out who this was because he could not see. I wonder, when you read these kinds of things, is your first impulse to think of Christ, or to think that the present author (me, and others) are completely stretching it?

The NT, not only in John, but also in Hebrews connects this all to Jesus. Read this familiar passage now through the eyes of the OT-NT logos theology. "Let us therefore strive to enter that rest, so that no one may fall by the same sort of disobedience. For the word of God is living and active, sharper than any two-edged sword, piercing to the division of soul and of spirit, of joints and of marrow, and discerning the thoughts and intentions of the heart. And no creature is hidden from his sight, but all are naked and exposed to the eyes of him to whom we must give account. Since then we have a great high priest who has passed through the heavens, Jesus, the Son of God, let us hold fast our confession" (Heb 4:11-14). Hebrews directly links the Word of God with Jesus, via the pronouns "him" and "his," rather than what we would expect if this was not a person: "it." The "word of God" in this passage is Christ.

In conclusion, we see the word of the LORD being called Yahweh by the texts, Adonai by the men, he stands, he touches with hands, he takes someone outside, and he walks through pieces of dead animals. Since the word of God and the Angel are so closely linked, we can now begin to make sense of how the Word is seen as embodied. Just like other angels that are not anthropomorphisms, or literary devices but real living entities, so also the Word of the LORD is the Angel of the LORD. In the NT, his name is Jesus, and he assumes human flesh. This is a teaser, for we will look at the Christ: The Name of God in the next chapter.

Study Questions:

1. What are the two ways "word" can be understood in the Bible?

2. What Greek term does the English "word" come from (John 1:1)?

3. What Jewish historian/philosopher contemporary with Christ, but who never heard of Jesus Christ, puts Word, Angel, Son, Image, Name, and Firstborn together?

4. What Aramaic term is equivalent to the English "word?"

5. In what manner did the "Word" come to Abraham (Gen 15:1)?

6. What name for God is equivalent for "Word" in Jeremiah 1:7?

7. What reason is given for Eli not being able to figure out that the Word was talking to Samuel (1 Sam 3:1-2)?

8. What pronoun is used of the "word of God" in Heb 4:13?

Part VIII

Christ: The Name of the LORD

Making a Name

Names are very important things in the Bible, and God has many of them: Yahweh/Jehovah, El, Elyon, and many, many more. Each name reveals something about God's character and attributes: El Shaddai (God of the Mountain), El Roi (God Who Sees), El Elyon (God Almighty), El Olam (Everlasting God), El Channun (Gracious God), Immanuel (God With Us), etc. But though he has many names, very early on in the Bible, God sets in motion a plan in response to the people at Babel who want "to make a name" for themselves (Gen 11:4). This plan is essentially to make (to glorify) a Name for himself. "Name" is the word *shem* in Hebrew, and through Noah's son Shem, the promised Seed will come (Gen 9:26-27). How might this work? Let's return to the idea of the Angel of the LORD.

Names of the Angel of the LORD

My favorite name for the Angel of the LORD in Jewish literature has to be Metatron (as opposed to Megatron, the evil leader of the Decepticons). No one quite knows its origin. Sometimes called "lesser Yahweh," some have suggested the possibility that the "him" in Ex 23:21 ("because my name is within <u>him</u> [the Angel]" refers to Metatron, where the *ttr* in the word comes from tetra, the word for "four" in Greek, and a shorthand for the Tetragrammaton word YHWH.[17]

With such luminary Protestants as Calvin, Isaac Watts, Charles Spurgeon, and Matthew Henry as well as OT scholars like Meredith Kline,[18] many through the centuries have suggested that a biblical proper name for this Angel is Michael. Michael is an archangel (Jude 9; Rev 12:7) of the heavenly council.[19] This council includes the heavenly angelic princes of Greece and Persia (Dan 10:20) and other "sons of God" (Ps 82:1). In Daniel, he is called "Michael your [Israel's] prince" (Dan 10:21) and "the great prince" (12:1).

Michael is a proper name. The name means "who is like God" (*mi-ka'el*). It can be either a statement or a question. If it is a statement, then it may point toward the direction that Michael is one who is like God. If it is a question, it might be read in light of Exodus 15:11, "Who is like you, O LORD among the gods (*mi-kamokah ba'elim yhwh*) ... doing wonders (*pele'*)?"

---

[17] See Andrei A. Orlov, *The Etymology of the Name 'Metatron,"* in *The Enoch-Metatron Tradition* (TSAJ, 107; Tuebiingen: Mohr-Sieback, 2005). An excerpt is here. See point #7: last accessed 8-14-2014.

[18] Calvin, Daniel 10:13; Watts, The Glory of Christ as God-Man 3.5; Spurgeon, The Angelic Life sermon 842; Kline, Kingdom Prologue Lecture 22.

[19] Also called the "divine council" (Ps 82:1), this is the group of heavenly beings (*elohim*) variously called the "sons of God" (Job 38:7; Ps 82:6) or "watchers" (Dan 4:17) who administer the affairs of the cosmos. Also 1 Kgs 22:13-23; Isa 6:1-9; Dan 7:9-14; etc. See Michael S. Heiser, "Divine Council," in Tremper Longman III and Peter Enns, eds., *Dictionary of the Old Testament: Wisdom, Poetry & Writings* (Downers Grove, IL; Nottingham, England: IVP Academic; Inter-Varsity Press, 2008).

There are a couple of lines to pursue here. First, let's look at the anatomy of this phrase in Exodus. When the Angel of the LORD appeared to Samson's mother and father, and he was asked his name, the Angel responded, "Why do you ask my name, seeing it is <u>Wonderful</u>?" (Jdg 13:18). This is similar to "doing wonders." It is interesting that the Angel phrases his response in the form of a question, just like the name Michael may be. This is of further interest in light of Isaiah 9:6 which predicts of the Messiah, "His name shall be called <u>Wonderful</u> (*pele'*), Counselor." Curiously, the LXX of this verse reads, "His name is called <u>the Angel of the great council</u>," and many Fathers used the LXX here to prove that Jesus was the Angel of the LORD before coming as a man. Thus, we can see from Ex 15:11, Jdg 13:18, and Isa 9:6 all have the idea of "wonder" in the name.

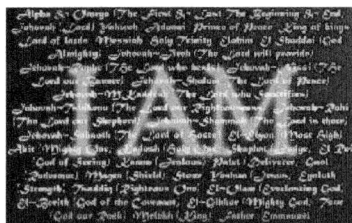

A second line of thought revolves around the two times the phrase "The LORD rebuke you" is found. In the first, "The Angel of the LORD" speaks these words to Satan (Zech 3:1-2). (In this passage, the "Angel of the LORD" and "Yahweh" are interchangeable). In the second, it is Michael who speaks these words to Satan (Jude 9), and this seems a deliberate echo, if not quote, from Zechariah.[20]

---

[20] See Richard J. Bauckham, *2 Peter, Jude*, vol. 50, Word Biblical Commentary (Dallas: Word, Incorporated, 1998), 65. Bauckham and many others do not take the view that Michael is the Angel.

Along these lines, we think about the only (other?) archangel mentioned in Scripture. The Apostle says, "For the Lord himself will descend from heaven with a cry of command, <u>with the voice</u> of an <u>archangel</u>, and with the sound of the trumpet of God. And <u>the dead in Christ will rise</u> first" (1 Th 4:16). While it could be that the Lord Jesus is distinct from the Archangel here, it could also be that he is the Archangel. Consider this amazing verse in light of something Jesus said, "Truly, truly, I say to you, an hour is coming, and is now here, when the dead will <u>hear the voice</u> of the <u>Son of God</u>, and <u>those who hear will live</u>." (John 5:25). With such similarities, it should be at least noted that while Michael is said to be "the great prince in charge of [God's] people" (Dan 12:1) and "[Israel's] prince" (Dan 10:21), that Israel is said to be Yahweh's, that is the Angel of the LORD's portion in Deuteronomy 32:9. Hence, the LORD in Deuteronomy is Michael in Daniel. This would make perfect sense if Michael is the proper name for the Angel, but it is difficult to reconcile if there are somehow two angels in charge of Israel. In the rest of this chapter, I want to focus on how the Name of the LORD actually becomes personified in much the same way that the Word does.

Name Personified

The NT refers to "names that are named" (Eph 1:21). In the verse, "names" is akin to "authorities," "powers," and "dominions," all titles of supernatural entities. So these entities are actually called "names." Often, in the same verse, we are commanded to praise "the LORD" and then the "name of the LORD" (Ps 113:1; 135:1; etc.). Similarly, we give thanks "to the LORD," and also to the "name of the LORD" (Ps 122:4). People are to fear "the LORD," but also "the name of the LORD" (Isa 59:19). The LORD is great, but then the Name is great (Jer 10:6). The same goes for trusting (Isa 50:10), loving (Isa 56:6), and glorifying (Isa 24:15). Normally we praise, thank, fear, trust, and love *people*. Therefore, the name of the LORD takes on a kind of identity all his own in these verses.[21]

Psalm 75:1 has the Psalmist rejoicing because God's name is near. Conversely, Isaiah 30:27 says, "Behold, the name of the LORD comes from afar, burning with his anger, and in thick rising smoke; his lips are full of fury, and his tongue is like a devouring fire." Here "angel" and "fury" are attributed to the name. This has lead scholars to summarize that, "God's name has become virtually an independent entity, separate from God, i.e. a hypostasis."[22] In my opinion, "Name" in these places should therefore be capitalized, as it often is in the great hymns of the faith:

> Immortal, invisible, God only wise,
> In light inaccessible hid from our eyes,
> Most blessed, most glorious, the Ancient of Days,
> Almighty, victorious, thy great <u>Name</u> we praise.

----

[21] In the grammar, "of the LORD" is a prepositional phrase. This means that the subject of "the Name of the LORD" is not "the LORD" but "the Name." "Of the LORD" modifies The Name.

[22] H. B. Huffmon, "Name," ed. Karel van der Toorn, Bob Becking, and Pieter W. van der Horst, *Dictionary of Deities and Demons in the Bible* (Leiden; Boston; Köln; Grand Rapids, MI; Cambridge: Brill; Eerdmans, 1999), 611.

We can see this from the NT. Nehemiah 9:5 says, "Blessed be your glorious name, which is exalted above all blessing and praise." The NT takes this passage and interprets it for us saying, "God has highly exalted him [Jesus] and bestowed on him the name that is above every name, so that at the name of Jesus every knee should bow, in heaven and on earth and under the earth" (Php 2:9-10).

All of this is what Exodus 23:21 means when it says of the Angel, "My Name is in him." "Name" becomes a way to have a piece of yourself into someone else, like when a father names his son after himself, thus calling him Jr. He biologically sires his son and then gives him the same name. The difference is, the Second Person of the Trinity is "eternally begotten."

Place of the Name

Finally, Moses says, "You shall seek the place that the LORD your God will choose out of all your tribes to put his Name and make his habitation there" (Deut 12:5). In the OT, this habitation was in the temple in Jerusalem. As we have seen in a previous chapter, Jesus now says he is the Temple (John 2:21). When you see "the name of the LORD," think about capitalizing it in your mind. Read it with Christ as the embodiment. For "Jesus" means "Ya [God] Saves" and "Christ" means "Anointed one." His name is Emmanuel—God with us. He is the place where atonement and life with God is carried out. He is the place of God's Name.

Study Questions:

1. What do God's names reveal about himself?

2. What have some Christians believed is a proper name for the Angel of the LORD? What does this name mean?

3. The terms "wonders" or "wonderful" are used of the Angel in what three passages as discussed in the chapter?

4. What are heavenly beings called in Ephesians 1:21?

5. What emotions are attributed to the Name by Isaiah?

6. What OT passage does Philippians 2:9-10 reflect upon?

7. In Deuteronomy 12:5, what is the place of God's Name?

PART IX
Christ: The Wisdom of God

The NT encourages us, "To reach all the riches of full assurance of understanding and the knowledge of God's mystery, which is <u>Christ,</u> in whom are hidden all the treasures of <u>wisdom</u> and knowledge" (Col 2:2-3). This comes on the heels of Jesus himself saying, "The queen of the South will rise up at the judgment with this generation and condemn it, for she came from the ends of the earth to hear the <u>wisdom of Solomon</u>, and behold, something <u>greater</u> than Solomon is here" (Matt 12:42), a passage we saw in our chapter on typology.

Solomon was of course known for his wisdom. God basically gave him one wish where he could have anything he wanted. "Ask what I shall give you" (2Ch 1:7), God said. "Give me now wisdom and knowledge" (10), was his answer. God (presumably the Angel) was very pleased with this response, because Solomon did not ask for "possessions, wealth, honor, or the life of those who hate you … or even long life" (11), or might I add like I probably would have done, a thousand more wishes(!). So, "God gave Solomon wisdom and understanding beyond measure …<u>Solomon's wisdom surpassed the wisdom of all the people of the east</u> and <u>all the wisdom of Egypt</u> … And people of all nations came to hear the wisdom of Solomon, and from all the kings of the earth, who had heard of his wisdom" (1Kgs 4:29, 30, 34). Somehow Christ is greater than this, but how?

A common way of answering this question is by demonstrating how wise Jesus actually was. Or, to put it another way, by going to the NT. Throughout his ministry, he was constantly outsmarting the Pharisees or teaching the Scripture with authority that no one else had. This is all true, of course, and necessary to know; but I have something else in mind in this chapter. This is a book on Christ in the Old Testament. So how might Christ be the Wisdom of God *in the OT*?

Wisdom at Creation

Let us remember that Solomon was the author of most of the Proverbs, including Proverbs 8. The end of this chapter has a rather extended and fascinating claim made by Wisdom:

22 The LORD possessed me at the beginning of his work, the first of his acts of old.
23 Ages ago I was set up, at the first, before the beginning of the earth.
24 When there were no depths I was brought forth, when there were no springs abounding with water.
25 Before the mountains had been shaped, before the hills, I was brought forth,
26 before he had made the earth with its fields, or the first of the dust of the world.
27 When he established the heavens, I was there; when he drew a circle on the face of the deep,
28 when he made firm the skies above, when he established the fountains of the deep,

²⁹ when he assigned to the sea its limit, so that the waters might not transgress his command, when he marked out the foundations of the earth,

³⁰ then I was beside him, like a master workman, and I was daily his delight, rejoicing before him always,

³¹ rejoicing in his inhabited world and delighting in the children of man.

(Prov 8:22-31)

Clearly, this does not refer to Solomon. But it does seem to refer to someone, that is to *a person.*

There are many fascinating correlations here to the creation episode of Genesis 1. Several words are found in both passages: beginning, the deep, water, sea, heaven, earth, and man. The Targum's interpretation of Genesis 1:1 seems to have Proverbs 8 in mind. "From the beginning <u>with wisdom</u> the <u>Memra</u> of the Lord created and perfected the heavens and the earth." Notice the link between the word ("Memra") and the wisdom of God. Almost all of the words we have been considering in these last chapters are related very closely in the texts, because they are all talking about the same Person. Combining the power and wisdom of God at creation, the Apostle says, "<u>Christ</u> [is] the <u>power</u> of God and the <u>wisdom</u> of God" (1 Cor 1:24).

Wisdom, the Law, and the Angel

Part of being wise is being able to properly discern and give proper judgment about God's law. In 2 Samuel it says, "But my lord the king is like the angel of God[23]; do therefore what seems good to you" (2Sa 19:27). The worldview here is important. It reflects the idea that God gave 70 heavenly sons of God to rule over the nations (Deut 32:7-8). They were supposed to rule with wisdom and justice. But they failed miserably (Ps 82:1-5). However, the Angel of the LORD does rule over Israel with wisdom and justice, and as the human king is the complement to the Angel on earth, he is likened to the Angel in heaven. David VanDrunen writes, "When human beings execute justice properly, Scripture sometimes likens them to angels. In addition to Psalm 8:5-6, in which the exercise of dominion places humans 'a little lower' than the angels, 2 Samuel 14:17 expresses this idea in the words of the wise woman who says to king David after he judges her case, 'my lord the king is like the angel of God to discern good and evil'" (underline added).[24]

Discerning good and evil takes us back to the Garden of Eden. As older English translations help us see, Satan's temptation was not to become "like God," but "like gods" (Gen

---

[23] This verse has the definite article "the." This is different from the two 2 Samuel verses listed below. However, the conceptual ideas are similar in that they surround wisdom and judgments. Therefore, the ESV has "the Angel..." in all three cases.

[24] David VanDrunen, *Divine Covenants and Moral Order: A Biblical Theology of Natural Law* (Grand Rapids, MI: Eerdmans, 2014), 541.

3:5 KJV, LXX), able to discern good from evil. In fact, Adam and Eve were given the responsibility to discern good from evil at that very moment, as the inspired commentary of Genesis 1-3—that is Psalm 19—explains. It is God's law, however, and not the voice of a fallen heavenly being, that is perfect, that makes wise the simple, that enlightens the eyes (Ps 19:7-9), all language that goes back to the Garden.

Satan, Adam, and Eve all sinned and did the opposite of discerning right and wrong. "Who can discern his errors," (12) the Psalm asks. Only God can keep our sins from having "dominion" (13), more language of the Garden.[25] Thankfully, the Angel of the LORD is the righteous, wise judge who never sins. Thus he is compared to the king, "In order to change the course of things your servant Joab did this. But my lord has wisdom like the wisdom of the angel of God to know all things that are on the earth" (2Sa 14:20).

Wisdom and Jesus

In the NT, Jesus tells the Pharisees, "Therefore also the Wisdom of God said, 'I will send them prophets and apostles, some of whom they will kill and persecute'" (Luke 11:49). No one knows if Jesus is referring to some lost text or to the whole OT (much the same way that Hebrews 11:33-38 does) when he brings up Wisdom saying this. But in the parallel account Jesus says, "Therefore I [Jesus] send you prophets

---

[25] For a short but fascinating discussion on this see D.J.A. Clines, "The Tree of Knowledge and the Law of Yawheh: Psalm XIX," *VT* 24 (1974), 8-14.

and wise men and scribes, some of whom you will kill and crucify, and some you will flog in your synagogues and persecute from town to town" (Matt 23:34). Comparing the two, Jesus sees himself as Wisdom, the one who revealed the future to us through prophecy and typology in the OT, the one who created the world.

In the next chapter, we will look at the strangely related idea of Christ as the Son of God in the OT. The next time you read through Proverbs or any other wisdom book, do more than think of it as wise and practical advice. Think of Christ as being both the Giver and Fulfiller of all that wisdom, for he is the Wisdom of God.

Study Questions:

1. What riches are said to be contained in Christ in Colossians 2:2-3?

2. What attribute more than any other is Solomon known for?

3. How is Wisdom described in Proverbs 8:30, and what was Wisdom doing in this passage?

4. With what do the Jewish Targum say the Lord created the world in Gen 1:1?

5. What is the job of the Angel in 2 Samuel 14:17?

6. What words are interchangeably "sending" in Luke 11:49 and Matthew 23:34?

PART X

Christ: The Son of God

In the NT, a phrase occurs identifying Jesus Christ as the "only begotten Son" of God (John 1:14, 18; 3:16; 1Jn 4:9). It is familiar enough, but its origins might not be. This exact Greek phrase does not appear in the OT LXX, so where might it come from? In this chapter we will look at two Psalms (Ps 2, 82) and Genesis 1 along with some NT reflections (John 10; Col 1) on these passages for an answer.

The most obvious place where we see something conceptually similar is Psalm 2:6-7. "I have set my King on Zion, my holy hill." I will tell of the decree: The LORD said to me, 'You are my <u>Son</u>; today I have <u>begotten</u> you'" This passage is cited several times by the NT as referring to Jesus (Acts 13:33; Heb 1:5; 5:5).

There is a fascinating and deliberate connection between this Psalm and Psalm 82. Consider these two verses: "Ask of me, and I will make the <u>nations</u> your <u>heritage</u>, and the ends of the earth your possession" (Ps 2:8). "Arise, O God, judge the earth; for you shall <u>inherit</u> all the <u>nations</u>!" (Ps 82:8). Psalm 2 has the Son inheriting the nations, while Psalm 82 has "God" inheriting them. The conceptual parallels between the two Psalms would suggest that the Son is God. This is actually what Psalm 82 means, as further reflection demonstrates.

Psalm 82:1 has "God" taking his place in something called "the divine council" (ESV), where "in the midst of the gods he holds judgment."[26] These "gods" are called "sons of God" in vs. 6, and when they judge badly, the foundations of the whole earth shake (vs. 5). The "sons of God" (*beney ha-elohom*) are the heavenly beings that were praising God while he was creating the universe (Job 38:7). In both the Bible and neighboring nations, they were considered God's heavenly royal family.[27]

Jesus cites Psalm 82:6 to the Pharisees (John 10:34-35). For a host of reasons[28] (not the least of which is the connection between Ps 2 and 82), the best interpretation of this passage is to see Jesus as claiming to be one of these heavenly beings. After all, he has "come down from heaven" (seven times in John 6). When he gives them this passage, it hardly alleviates their anger at his blasphemy, either. This is why they still want to

---

[26] I realize there is controversy among Evangelicals surrounding the identification of these "gods." For definitive reasons why they cannot refer to humans see Cyrus Gordon, "אלהים (Elohim) in Its Reputed Meaning of Rulers, Judges," *Journal of Biblical Literature* 54 (1935): 139–144; W. S. Prinsloo, "Psalm 82: Once Again, Gods or Men?" *Biblica* 76:2 (1995): 219–228; Lowell Handy, "Sounds, Words and Meanings in Psalm 82," *Journal for the Study of the Old Testament* 47 (1990), 51–66; Michael S. Heiser, "Deuteronomy 32:8 and the Sons of God," *Bibliotheca Sacra* 158:629 (Jan-Mar, 2001): 60-72 [52-74].

[27] I have written about this in the Introduction to my book Giants: Sons of the Gods. There is a host of other literature that delves into this as well. Perhaps the best place to be introduced to this whole fascinating subject is the Divine Council website of Dr. Michael Heiser who did his dissertation on the subject.

[28] See Michael S. Heiser, "You've Seen One Elohim, You've Seen Them All? A Critique of Mormonism's Use of Psalm 82," *FARMS Review* 19/1 (2007): 221–266.

kill him after he quotes the verse. Yet, John 10 makes it clear that Jesus is also different from the other sons of God, for he has a unique relationship to the Father. He is "in" the Father and the Father is "in" him (John 10:34:36-38). No other being can say this. Psalm 2 is the same idea, except it uses the term "begotten."

The NT comes along and uses the word "only begotten" (*monogenes*) and applies it to Jesus. This word means "unique" or "one of a kind," as is easily seen by the fact that Isaac is the "only begotten" son of Abraham (Heb 11:17), even though Abraham had Ishmael 13 years earlier (I think it is actually a double entendra, as it can also mean in some sense, "begotten"[29]). Thus, anytime we see "sons of God" or even "gods" in the OT, our thought should go to the unique Son of God, the one who created any others who "may be called gods" (1 Cor 8:5).

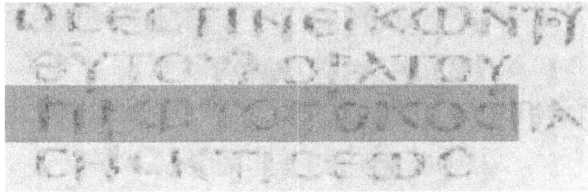

[29] On "begotten" see Lee Irons, "The Eternal Generation of the Son," last accessed 8-15-2014. Basically, two etymologies have been proposed for *monogenes*. "Gennao" (Ps 2:7 LXX) means "to bear, beget." "Genos" means "unique, class, kind." There may even be a triple entendre going on with this word, as it has very close affinities with "beloved" (as in God's beloved son; Matt 3:17; 17:5; Mark 1:11; 9:7; Luke 3:22; 20:13). "Monogenes," Gerhard Kittel, Geoffrey W. Bromiley, and Gerhard Friedrich, eds., *Theological Dictionary of the New Testament* (Grand Rapids, MI: Eerdmans, 1964–), 739.

Speaking of this creation, in Colossians 1:15-18, the Apostle Paul, reflecting upon creation and Genesis 1 (we talked about this in the previous chapter) explains, "He is the <u>image</u> of the invisible God, the <u>firstborn</u> of all creation" (15). "God" seems to refer to the Father here. The word "firstborn" is the word *prototokos*. It comes up again in vs. 18 where it says, "And he is the head of the body, the church. He is the <u>beginning,</u> the <u>firstborn</u> (*prototokos*) from the dead, that in everything he might be preeminent." But Paul has not given up his treatment of creation in between these two verses, much less is he saying that this firstborn was created. For he says, "For <u>by him</u> [the firstborn] all things were <u>created,</u> in <u>heaven</u> and on earth, visible and <u>invisible,</u> whether <u>thrones</u> or <u>dominions</u> or <u>rulers</u> or <u>authorities</u>—<u>all</u> things were created through him and for him. And he is before all things, and in him all things hold together" (16-17). Notice how predominate the creation of heavenly beings is in this text.

"But who is this "he," this "firstborn," this "beginning?" Proverbs 8 called him "Wisdom," and this is the connection to our previous chapter. But here, he is deliberately called "His beloved Son" (13). What is amazing about this is how the Church Fathers knew of translations of Genesis 1:1 that went this way: "In the beginning, God became a Son" or "In the beginning, God made for himself a Son."[30] Depending on the exact Greek terms, these may or may not be heretical ideas. However, the Latin Father Jerome states the opinion of people saying, "Most people think that in the Hebrew is con-

---

[30] See Tertullian, *Against Praxeas* 5.1.

tained 'In the Son, God made heaven and earth.'"[31] So whereas the Targum said God created the earth through his Word in Wisdom, this idea has God doing it through the Firstborn Son. This is perfectly orthodox, but how could anyone possibly get this from Genesis 1:1?

The word *reshith* can mean either "beginning" (as most people understand it, i.e. "in the beginning..."), or "first," or even the idea of a "firstborn" in Hebrew (cf. Gen 49:3). Thus, the Bible in Basic English reads, "At the first God made the heaven and the earth" (Gen 1:1 BBE). In English, "first" can have the idea of either time or rank (the same is true in Greek and Hebrew). If I say, "She was the first in class," I could mean either that she was the first to arrive to the classroom (time), or that she was had the best grades in his class (rank; in my experience, girls were usually first in rank or grades). Paul may in fact have this idea in mind and may be capitalizing on it in Colossians, though as John 1:1's "in the beginning" shows, this would clearly be seen as a flexible idea. So it is strangely possible to translate Genesis 1:1 with the firstborn in mind, even as we have seen that it also includes ideas of the word and wisdom as well. All of this relates to Christ as the Son of God. The NT is not making the idea that Christ is the only begotten Son of God up. It is getting it from the OT.

---

[31] Jerome, Questions in *Hebrew, in Genesis i. 507. Quoted in Saint Jerome's Hebrew Questions on Genesis*, trans. C.T. R. Hayward (Oxford: Oxford University Pres, 195), 30.

In the next chapter, we will look at Christ: The Glory of God.

Study Questions:

1. What famous adjective(s) is used of God's Son in John 3:16?

2. What does Psalm 2:7 say about the Son?

3. What two figures inherit the nations in Psalm 2:8 and 82:8?

4. Who are the "sons of God" in Job 38:7 and Psalm 82:1, 6?

5. What is Jesus claiming by quoting Psalm 82:6 in John 10:34 that makes the Pharisees still want to kill Jesus for blasphemy?

6. What does *monogenes* ("begotten") mean in Heb 11:17?

7. What word found in Col 1:18 can be substituted for "beginning" in Genesis 1:1?

8. Are "Son" and "Firstborn" interchangeable in Colossians 1:13-18?

PART XI
Christ: The Glory of God

Most people probably think of the glory (Heb. *kabod*; Gk. *doxa*) of God in a very abstract sense, like God's reputation or his honor. "Glory" literally means "to be weighty, full of good things." Certainly "praise" is not far removed from glory either. Each of these are good and right to ascribe to the glory of God. But this is, again, a book on Christ in the OT, and we are going to take a look at how the glory of God is especially related to him.

A good place to start is with Moses. At one point he asks, "Please show me your <u>glory</u>" (Ex 33:18). The glory of the LORD appears in only a couple of places prior to this. In Exodus 16:10, "The glory of the LORD appeared <u>in</u> the cloud." The glory is not the cloud, but is *in* the cloud. It is difficult to see how or why this would be talking about God's honor or praise due him. We see the same thing eight chapters later when, "The <u>glory</u> of the LORD rested on Mount Sinai, and the <u>cloud</u> covered it for six days; and on the seventh day <u>He</u> called to Moses <u>from the midst of the cloud</u>" (24:16). "He?" We believe the "he" here refers to the Glory, for again, the glory and cloud are separate, and he is calling from inside the cloud.

Before discovering what Moses is actually asking for (and what God gives him in response), consider a couple more things from earlier in Exodus. First, as we saw with the Angel of the LORD, Moses has been talking to the Angel. This angel has been shrouded in flame (Ex 3:2) and in a cloud. "The angel of God … moved and went behind them, and the pillar of cloud moved from before them and stood behind them" (Ex 14:19). Just before this, it says that "the LORD" went before them "in a pillar of cloud … and by night in a pillar of fire" (13:21). Just like the glory, the LORD is in the cloud. On Mount Sinai, "The LORD" promised, "Behold, I am coming to you in a thick cloud" (Ex 19:9). As we have seen, "The glory of the LORD dwelt on Mount Sinai, and the cloud covered it…" (24:16).

The word "dwelt" here is important. It is the verb *shakan*. It is from this that the famous "Shekinah" derives. Shekinah is not a biblical word, but it is found throughout the Aramaic Targums as another buffer word (like Memra/word or Name).[32] Thus, "Jacob awoke from his sleep and said, 'Surely the LORD is in this place, and I did not know it'" (Gen 28:16) becomes, "The Glory of the Lord's Shekinah dwells in this place, and I knew it not. (Gen 28:16 PJE). "Moses hid his face, for he was afraid to look at God" (Ex 3:6) becomes, "He

---

[32] One Bible dictionary says, "In the later rabbinic sources does the Shekinah become a separate entity created by God as an intermediary between God and man." The same dictionary says, "In the Targums 'shekinah,' 'glory of God,' and 'word of God' are used synonymously. "Glory," in Walter A. Elwell and Barry J. Beitzel, *Baker Encyclopedia of the Bible* (Grand Rapids, MI: Baker Book House, 1988), 1943.

was afraid to look upon the height of the <u>glory</u> of the <u>Shekinah</u> of the Lord" (Ex 3:6 JPE). This last one is interesting for us, because we have seen that it is the Angel of the LORD Moses is afraid to look at.

Now, earlier in Exodus 33, it tells us that Moses entered into the tent and the pillar of cloud would descend and stand at the entrance, and the LORD would speak to Moses (33:9). "The LORD descended in the <u>cloud</u> and <u>stood</u> with him there, and <u>proclaimed</u> the <u>name</u> of the LORD" (34:5). (Recall our discussion of The Name). Two things here. First, Numbers 12:8 tells us, "With him I speak mouth to mouth, clearly, and not in riddles, and he beholds <u>the form</u> [Heb: *temunah*] <u>of the LORD</u>." The form of the LORD? The Greek translates "form" here as *doxa* or "glory."

Second, there would later be a place where the LORD will choose "to make his <u>name</u> <u>dwell</u> there" (Deut 16:2). And yet, the Psalm says, "O LORD, I love the habitation of your house and the place where your <u>glory</u> <u>dwells</u>" (Ps 26:8). We see this emerge clearly in the dedication of the temple by Solomon. First, they bring the ark (God's throne-seat) to the Most Holy Place inside the newly built temple (1 Kgs 8:6). Then, the "cloud" fills the house of the LORD (10). The

LORD now lives here in a special sense, even though the highest heavens cannot contain him. Then, the <u>cloud</u> and <u>glory</u> are linked as God's presence (11). Solomon recognizes that God will dwell in his temple, though the universe cannot contain him (27). Finally, the LORD appears to Solomon (9:1) telling him that now his "<u>name</u> is there" (3). We are supposed to understand from this that the Name is the Glory veiled by the cloud.[33]

One more OT prophet is important to look at here. Ezekiel see the "<u>likeness</u> as the <u>appearance</u> of a <u>man</u>" (Ezek 1:26). He looked like gleaming metal and his lower body was like fire. He concludes, "This was the <u>appearance</u> of the <u>likeness</u> of the <u>Glory</u> of the LORD" (28). Later in the book, the Glory is the LORD (Ezek 9:3-4).

The NT says some pretty amazing things about all this. "And the <u>Word</u> became flesh and <u>dwelt</u> among us, and we have seen his <u>glory</u>, glory as of the only <u>Son</u> from the Father, full of grace and truth" (John 1:14). John equates the *logos*, the glory, and the Son. They are all the same thing. It is into this Glory as a Person idea that John later writes, "Isaiah saw his

---

[33] Meredith Kline believes that the Shekinah-glory is the Holy Spirit ("Kingdom Prologue, Lecture 14," 2012, p. 2; last accessed 8-16-2014. He is close. It is better to see the cloud and fire as images of the Spirit who then enshrouds the Word-Angel-Glory-Name person inside. This is the way the Revelator saw it, "Then I saw another mighty <u>angel</u> coming down from heaven, wrapped <u>in a cloud</u>" (Rev 10:1).

Glory" (Isa 12:41).[34] Read epexegetically, Acts 7:55 may very well say, "He [Stephen] … saw the <u>glory</u> of God, <u>that is</u> <u>Jesus</u> standing at the right hand of God."

And then there is Philippians 2:6-11. Christ exists "in the <u>form</u> of God" and the "<u>likeness</u> of men" (6-7). Recall that Moses beheld the "form [Heb: *temunah*; GK: *doxa*] of the LORD." The Hebrew word was translated as "glory" by the LXX, but that same Hebrew word is translated as "likeness" (*homoioma*) in the Second Commandment (Ex 20:4). This happens to be the word used for "likeness" in Php 2:7. The old hymn here is not saying that Christ only appeared to be one of us, but really wasn't. Rather, it is saying that he is the Glory of God. Thus one dictionary notes, "'Taking the form of a slave', 'becoming in the likeness of men'; and 'being found in the fashion as a man' (vv 7-8) … Phil 2:6 would seem to say that Christ is the divine Glory. The same idea is expressed by the title, 'image of the invisible God"; in the beginning of the hymn of Christ in Col 1:15-20).[35]

In light of all this, it seems to me that Moses was not asking to see the Father (whom Jesus says no man has seen, or can see). He was asking to see the face of the preincarnate Second

---

[34] Isaiah 6:1, "I saw the Lord (*Adonai*)" becomes "I saw the <u>glory</u> of the LORD" (6:1 Isaiah Targum), which becomes, "Mine eyes have seen the <u>glory</u> of the <u>She-kinah</u> of the King of the worlds, the <u>Lord of hosts</u>" (Isa 6:5 IST).

[35] J. E. Fossum, "Glory," ed. Karel van der Toorn, Bob Becking, and Pieter W. van der Horst, *Dictionary of Deities and Demons in the Bible* (Leiden; Boston; Köln; Grand Rapids, MI; Cambridge: Brill; Eerdmans, 1999), 351 [348-52]. This entire entry is extremely helpful in grounding our discussion.

Person, in whom he was trusting (Heb 11:26); unshrouded from the cloud and fire (and the angel?). God granted that he might see his unshrouded backside, but not his face. Think about this. Moses asks to see God's glory, and he shows him his "backside." Not an abstract idea or an anthropomorphism, but a person. The glory and the person are mysteriously united together.

In some ways, it is very similar to the transfiguration of Christ on the mountain, where curiously Moses also appeared. Peter says, "When he received honor <u>and glory</u> from God the Father, and the voice was borne to him by the <u>Majestic Glory</u>, 'This is my beloved Son, with whom I am well pleased,' we ourselves heard this very voice borne from heaven, for we were with him on the holy mountain" (2Pe 1:17-18). The Glory of the Second Person is omnipresent, but that same Glory is now fully contained in the Person of Jesus Christ. He is the new equivalent of the OT Glory.

In the incarnation, God who said, "'Let light <u>shine</u> out of darkness,' has <u>shone</u> in our hearts to give the light of the knowledge of the <u>glory of God</u> <u>in the face of Jesus Christ</u>" (2 Cor 4:6). "Arise, <u>shine,</u> for your light has come, and <u>the glory</u> of the LORD has <u>risen</u> upon you" (Isa 60:1). "Therefore it says, 'Awake, O sleeper, and <u>arise</u> from the dead, and <u>Christ</u> will <u>shine</u> on you'" (Eph 5:14).

Study Questions:

1. What does "glory" mean?

2. In Exodus 16:10, where was the glory located?

3. What pronoun is used of "glory" in Exodus 24:16?

4. What Aramaic word is synonymous with "glory?"

5. What does Moses behold in Num 12:8 and what Greek word is used in the LXX for it?

6. What words are interchangeable to describe the "appearance" the prophet saw in Ezekiel 1:26 and 28?

7. What did they behold in John 1:14?

8. What person was Moses asking to see when he asked to see God's glory?

PART XII

Christ: The Right Arm of God

"Who has believed what he has heard from us? And to whom has <u>the arm of the LORD</u> been revealed?" asks the prophet (Isa 53:1), as he begins his lengthy and mysterious prophecy of the Suffering Servant which is probably the high water mark for all Messianic prophecies in the OT. The arm or right hand of the LORD will be the last term we will look at in this book that we can equate with the Angel of the LORD. Like several in the list, this one is easy to misunderstand.

When people think of the "arm" of the LORD, many probably anthropomorphize the idea. God doesn't literally have an arm, anymore than he literally has eyes or wings. God is Spirit. Of course, we wholeheartedly agree with this, in as much as we are talking about the One Being called God. However, when the Bible speaks of God's arm or his right hand (see Deut 4:34; 9:29; 26:8), it has something more concrete in mind than merely symbolizing God vis-à-vis personification.

The "right hand" in the ancient world was a way of describing a position or seat of great authority and power that a particular individual, such as a general or captain, holds under the command of the king. We saw previously how the he commander of the LORD's army (Josh 15:14; cf. Ex 15:3) identified himself as the Angel of the LORD to Joshua saying, "Take off your sandals from your feet, for the place where you are standing is holy" (Josh 5:15, cf. Ex 3:5). In the NT, God seated Christ "at his right hand in the heavenly places, far above all rule and authority and power and dominion, and above every name that is named" (Eph 1:20-21), after he "disarmed" and "triumphed over them" (Col 2:15), having made them subject to him (1 Pet 3:22). This refers to Jesus' victory as King of kings and Lord of lords.

The arm of the LORD is a way of talking about this commander or this right hand. We can see that the arm and right hand of God are related in the same way a human hand and arm are related by not identical. "You have a mighty arm; strong is your hand, high your right hand" (Ps 89:13). The arm seems to be what the right hand (man) carries out. The arm stands for military power (Deut 4:34; Isa 30:30), creative power (Isa 51:9; Ps 89:11, 14),[36] and God as a judge (Isa 51:5).

Let's take a more detailed look now at the arm as it is described in the Exodus, especially as it regards salvation and judgment. The first verse describing it says, "I will redeem you with an outstretched arm" (Ex 6:6). We find this salvation theme with the right hand and/or arm in other places as

---

[36] These texts combine the original creation and God's mythical battle with the sea monster from pagan stories with the new creation God is doing in his military battle at the Exodus as he assaults and defeats Rahab, the Egyptian-Pharaonic "sea monster." For more on the connection to the Exodus, Pharaoh, and how the arm is "the vehicle by which he conquers see J. K. Hoffmeier, "The Arm of God versus the Arm of Pharaoh in the Exodus Narratives," Bib 67 (1986): 378–87; last accessed 8-29-2014.

well (Ps 98:1; Isa 33:2; 52:10). Moses then sings of the beginning of this prophetic fulfillment, "Terror and dread fall upon them; because of the <u>greatness of your arm</u>, they are still as a stone, till your people, O LORD, pass by, till the people pass by <u>whom you have purchased</u>" (Ex 15:16). Who shall do this? "The LORD is <u>a man of war</u>; the LORD is his Name" (15:3). (Notice again the "Name" theme). Moses sees the arm of the LORD as the man of war, Yahweh, the angel of Yahweh, who is later called the LORD of Hosts or Armies (Hos 12:4-5).

Isaiah reflects on this very same thing and says, "Where is he who brought them up out of the sea with the shepherds of his flock? Where is he who put in the midst of them his Holy Spirit, who caused his <u>glorious arm</u> to go at the right hand of

Moses, who divided the waters before them to make for himself an everlasting <u>name</u>" (Isa 63:11-12). This time we can see the relationship between the arm and the name. But dictionaries are very provocative when they boldly assert things like, "'Arm' is used as a <u>hypostasis</u> in Isa 63:12. Here the *zeroa* stands for an independent power going side by side with Moses and stressing the function of

Yhwh as Shepherd and leader of his people."[37] "Hypostasis" is exactly how Christians describe the divine and human natures in the One Person of Jesus Christ (the hypostatic union) and the relationship between the Father, Son, and Holy Spirit (Three *Hypostases*) to the Godhead (in one *Ousia*). We've seen this idea now with the Word, the Name, and the Glory.

Into this theology, the last chapter of the Bible has Jesus himself saying, "Behold, I am coming soon, bringing my recompense with me, to repay each one for what he has done" (Rev 22:12). This is a paraphrase of Isaiah 40:10 and the Messianic prophecy that says, "Behold, the Lord GOD (*Adonai Yahweh*) comes with might, and his arm rules for him; behold, his reward is with him, and his recompense before him." Thus, Greg Beale concludes, "What is prophesied of the Lord in Isaiah is now prophesied by Jesus to be fulfilled by himself."[38] No wonder then that Jude says Jesus saved a people out of the land of Egypt (Jude 1:5, see Christ in the OT Part II).

Thus, in answer to the original question of this chapter, John's Gospel says, "Though he had done so many signs before them, they still did not believe in him, so that the word spoken by the prophet Isaiah might be fulfilled: "Lord, who has believed what he heard from us, and to whom has the

---

[37] B. Becking, "Arm," ed. Karel van der Toorn and Pieter W. van der Horst, *Dictionary of Deities and Demons in the Bible* (Leiden; Boston; Köln; Grand Rapids, MI; Cambridge: Brill; Eerdmans, 1999), 90.

[38] G. K. Beale and D. A. Carson, *Commentary on the New Testament Use of the Old Testament* (Grand Rapids, MI; Nottingham, UK: Baker Academic; Apollos, 2007), 1156.

<u>arm of the Lord</u> been revealed?" (John 12:37-38). Indeed, Jesus is the Arm the LORD, the great military commander who carries out justice on the earth, and who powerfully saves his people.

But the people were wrong in their view of him. They thought he would be a military commander who would crush the head of the Roman beast. Instead, Isaiah predicted this salvation would come through a great twist of irony. The Arm of the LORD would be revealed through the Suffering Servant. He would win the victory alright, but it would be a victory over sin, death, and the devil by suffering and dying for our sins and being raised from the dead. Truly, his Right Arm is Glorious.

Study Questions:

1. In the ancient world, what does the "right hand" describe?

2. How is the Angel described in Joshua 5:14 and Exodus 15:3?

3. Where is Christ seated at his ascension (Eph 1:20-21; 1 Pet 3:22)?

4. In Psalm 89:13, what does the mighty hand stand for?

5. How does God redeem in Exodus 6:6?

6. What term that we use to describe the union between Christ's human and divine natures did we say is also used to describe the glorious arm in Isaiah 63:11-12?

7. Revelation 22:12 borrows from Isaiah 40:10 and replaces "his arm" with what person?

PART XIII

Conclusion

Throughout this book, we have looked at how Jesus gives us his own key for interpreting the Bible. This key is to see him in all the Scripture. When a person does this, it is the key to life itself, for it opens the way by which we may come to him. We have seen many NT passages that explicitly teach that Jesus was in the OT. We have learned how prophecy, typology, and the law each point to him in their own unique ways. We have also seen how there are certain words and ideas that profoundly and mysteriously describe an actual person in the OT, a person who is present with his people, who walks among them, who fights for them, who delivers them, who covenants with them, but who had not yet come in the flesh. We have seen seven ideas, that he is the Angel, the Word, the Name, the Wisdom, The Son, the Glory, and the Arm of the LORD.

None of these are original to me; all have been written about by scholars, in journals, books, Bible dictionaries, etc. to one degree or another. Also, it isn't that in this book we are somehow saying that all prophecy is about Christ in the same way, or that there is no such thing as anthropomorphism in this list of words (sure there are, we can think of each of these in the more abstract senses too), etc. But rather that in some ways, Christ is related to all of these things. Not in every way, but in some ways. We are not presenting an either/or, but a both/and. We just happen to be talking about Christ at this time.

To conclude this thought I want to turn to Hebrews. Hebrews speaks of prophets, types, and law all in the context of Jesus fulfilling them. But in an absolutely fascinating opening to this book-sermon, Hebrews does something amazing with all of the individual words we have been looking at. It begins by telling us how Christ is superior to angels. After writing most of these chapters, I was flabbergasted to discover that we find all seven of these word-ideas being applied to Christ in the span of just five verses. "In these last days [God] has spoken to us by his Son" (Heb 1:2). "He is the radiance of the glory of God" (1:3). "He upholds the universe by the word of his power" (1:3). "He sat down at the right hand of the Majesty on high" (1:3). "Having become as much superior to angels as the name he has inherited is more excellent than theirs" (1:4). "When the brings the firstborn[39] into the world, he says, 'Let all God's angels worship him'" (1:6). If we add the first verse of the book, we can add the first three categories we talked about (prophecy, typology, law): "Long ago, at many times and in many ways, God spoke to our fathers by the prophets" (Heb 1:1).

Whoever wrote this letter, "got it." Of course he did! He was inspired by God himself. But he also interpreted the Scripture

---

[39] Recall our discussion of "first" and "firstborn" in the chapter on Wisdom and then the chapter on the Son.

using the basic principle that Jesus taught him. Clearly, the original authors knew and applied each of this ideas to Christ. Their hearts were saturated with seeing him as is was in the OT, and as he became at his incarnation.

I hope that this book has shown that learning to see Christ in the OT is both a science and an art. It takes knowledge, desire, and practice. The more you do it, the better you should get. Nevertheless, it is not always easy to do this correctly, and many have made mistakes. In fact, all of us have. Some have seen Christ where he probably is not. By not using sound rules of interpretation, by wanting to see things that aren't there, or by not understanding that there is more than one way to see Christ in the OT, they have not interpreted the Scripture as best they could. But others—sadly many others—have failed to see him where he clearly is, often in many, many places where he is to be found in the OT, in places that I believe OT peoples would themselves have had at least an inkling of some kind of plurality in a kind of God-head.

People often ask me about this. "Then who should try?" Well, we all "try," no matter if we try to see him or don't are to see him at all. So putting into practice this question is unavoidable. The question is, will you follow the Savior's hermeneutic, or one of your own making?

This can be a frightening business, for who wants to misinterpret God's word? I've often told people that on The Day I face the LORD in judgment, he may very well ask me how I handled his word. Perhaps he would ask me one of two questions. The first, "Doug, why did you see my Son in places he was not?" The second, "Doug, why did not you see my Son in places where he is to be found?" As for me, I guess I would much rather err by seeing too much of the Savior than not enough, especially given his own explicit teaching on this subject, and the reprimand he gave the ordinary (non-Apostolic) disciple Cleopas and his unnamed friend on the road to Emmaus. He expected they would do this. I do not desire to read and teach the Bible as an end to itself. The Pharisees read it in just this way, and would not come to Christ to have life (John 5:40).

How about you?

Works Cited

Baker Encyclopedia of the Bible. Ed. Walter A. Elwell and Barry J. Beitzel. Grand Rapids, MI: Baker Book House, 1988.

Bauckham, Richard. "The Throne of God and the Worship of Jesus." In *The Jewish Roots of Christological Monotheism: Papers from the St. Andrews Conference on the Historical Origins of the Worship of Jesus*. Ed. C. Newman, J. Davila, and G. Lewis. Leiden: E. J. Brill, 1999.

Becking, B. "Arm." In *Dictionary of Deities and Demons in the Bible*. Ed. Karel van der Toorn and Pieter W. van der Horst. Leiden; Boston; Köln; Grand Rapids, MI; Cambridge: Brill; Eerdmans, 1999.

Bruce, F. F. *The Epistle to the Galatians: a Commentary on the Greek Text*, New International Greek Testament Commentary. Grand Rapids, MI: W.B. Eerdmans Pub. Co., 1982.

Boyarin, Daniel. "The Gospel of the Memra: Jewish Binitarianism and the Prologue to John." *Harvard Theological Review* 94:3 (2001): 243-84.

Calvin, John. *Commentary on Genesis*.

Cathcart, Kevin; Maher, Michael; and McNamara, Martin eds. *The Aramaic BibleA: Targum Neofiti 1: Genesis*, trans. Martin McNamara, vol. 1. Collegeville, MN: The Liturgical Press, 1992.

Clines, D.J.A. "The Tree of Knowledge and the Law of Yawheh: Psalm XIX." *VT* 24 (1974): 8-14.

Commentary on the New Testament Use of the Old Testament. Ed. G. K. Beale and D. A. Carson. Grand Rapids, MI; Nottingham, UK: Baker Academic; Apollos, 2007.

Edwards, M. J. "Justine's Logos and the Word of God." *JECS* 3 (1995): 261-80.

Fossum, J. E. "Glory." In *Dictionary of Deities and Demons in the Bible*. Ed. Karel van der Toorn, Bob Becking, and Pieter W. van der Horst. Leiden; Boston; Köln; Grand Rapids, MI; Cambridge: Brill; Eerdmans, 1999.

Gordon, Cyrus. "אלהים (Elohim) in Its Reputed Meaning of Rulers, Judges." *Journal of Biblical Literature* 54 (1935): 139–144.

Goulder, Michael. *Midrash and Lection in Matthew: The Speaker's Lectures in Biblical Studies, 1969-71*. London: SPCK, 1974.

Heiser, Michael S. "Deuteronomy 32:8 and the Sons of God," *Bibliotheca Sacra* 158:629 (Jan-Mar, 2001): 52-74.

_____. "Divine Council," in Tremper Longman III and Peter Enns, eds., *Dictionary of the Old Testament: Wisdom, Poetry & Writings*. Downers Grove, IL; Nottingham, England: IVP Academic; Inter-Varsity Press, 2008.

_____. *The Myth That is True*. Unpublished.

_____. "Why Use the Septuagint." LogosTalk (Dec 2007). https://blog.logos.com/2007/12/why_use_the_septuagint/, last accessed 5-4-2015.

_____. "You've Seen One Elohim, You've Seen Them All? A Critique of Mormonism's Use of Psalm 82." *FARMS Review* 19/1 (2007): 221–266.

Hendriksen, William and Kistemaker, Simon J. *Exposition of the Gospel According to Matthew*, vol. 9. New Testament Commentary. Grand Rapids: Baker Book House, 1953–2001.

Hoffmeier, J. K. "The Arm of God versus the Arm of Pharaoh in the Exodus Narratives." *Bib* 67 (1986): 378–87.

Huffmon, H. B. "Name." In *Dictionary of Deities and Demons in the Bible*. Ed. Karel van der Toorn, Bob Becking, and Pieter W. van der Horst. Leiden; Boston; Köln; Grand Rapids, MI; Cambridge: Brill; Eerdmans, 1999.

Hurtado, Larry. "The Binitarian Shape of Early Christian Worship." *In The Jewish Roots of Christological Monotheism: Papers from the St. Andrews Conference on the Historical Origins of the Worship of Jesus.* Ed. C. Newman, J. Davila, and G. Lewis. Leiden: E. J. Brill, 1999.

Irons, Lee. "The Eternal Generation of the Son." http://www.upper-register.com/papers/monogenes.html. Last accessed 8-15-2014.

Kline, Meredith G. "Kingdom Prologue, Lecture 14." 2012. https://faculty.gordon.edu/hu/bi/ted_hildebrandt/digitalcourses/kline_kingdomprologue/kline_kingdom_prologue_text/kline_kingdomprologue_lecture14.pdf. Last Accessed 8-16-2014.

Metzger, Bruce Manning. *A Textual Commentary on the Greek New Testament, Second Edition a Companion Volume to the United Bible Societies' Greek New Testament (4th Rev. Ed.).* United Bible Societies. London; New York: United Bible Societies, 1994.

Orlov, Andrei A. *The Etymology of the Name 'Metatron," in The Enoch-Metatron Tradition.* TSAJ, 107; Tuebiingen: Mohr-Sieback, 2005.

Pao David W., and Schnabel, Eckhard J. "Luke." In *Commentary on the New Testament Use of the Old Testament.* Ed. G. K. Beale and D. A. Carson. Grand Rapids, MI; Nottingham, UK: Baker Academic; Apollos, 2007.

Prinsloo, W. S. "Psalm 82: Once Again, Gods or Men?" *Biblica* 76:2 (1995): 219–228.

Segal, Alan F. *Two Powers in Heaven: Early Rabbinic Reports about Christianity and Gnosticism.* SJLA 25. Leiden: E. J. Brill, 1977.

Theological Dictionary of the New Testament. Kittel, Gerhard; Bromiley, Geoffrey W.; and Friedrich, Gerhard eds. Grand Rapids, MI: Eerdmans, 1964– .

Van Dorn, Douglas. *Giants: Sons of the Gods.* Erie, CO: Waters of Creation Publishing, 2013.

_____. *Waters of Creation: A Biblical-Theological Study of Baptism.* Erie, Co: Waters of Creation Pub., 2009.

VanDrunen, David. *Divine Covenants and Moral Order: A Biblical Theology of Natural Law*. Grand Rapids, MI: Eerdmans, 2014.

Vos, Geerhardus. *Biblical Theology*. Grand Rapids, MI: Eerdmans, 1948.

Welty, Greg. "Eschatological Fulfillment and the Confirmation of Mosaic Law." http://www.the-highway.com/mosaic-law_Welty.html. Last accessed, 8-14-2014.

Also cited:

Church Fathers: Justin Martyr, Pseudo-Ignatius, Irenaeus, Tertullian, Cyprian, Novatian, Eusebius, Athanasius, Hilary of Poitiers, Gregory Nazianzen, Basil, Ambrose, Chrysostom, Augustine, Jerome, Cyril, Socrates Scholasticus, Constitutions of the Holy Apostles.

Jewish: Philo, Josephus, Genesis Rabbah, and the Babylonian Talmud.

All pictures are found in the public domain.

Printed in Great Britain
by Amazon

59524447R00066